To
Mike & Beryl
from
Jerry & Janis
Christmas 1984

Perhaps more than anything else, Bend's early history is that of a town that was born, was nurtured and has matured as a community built around timber and timber production.

But as this history has continued to define itself, this lovely community with its delightful mix of the high desert and pristine pine forests has developed many other special characteristics that make it unique.

Throughout Oregon, and in some cases throughout the Northwest, the mention of Bend evokes fond memories in the minds of the thousands of vacationers who have enjoyed its hospitality and unparalleled recreational opportunities.

And Bend itself is in many circles the envy of those who live and work in other parts of our great state. To many of our fellow Oregonians, the chance to make a life in Bend has become an enduring dream.

For those of us who are fortunate enough to live and work here, we pay tribute to Bend's history, which is recent by our nation's standards, but equally as significant. We appreciate the contributions of those pioneers who came before, and, as we now do for those who will follow, made possible the heritage we have.

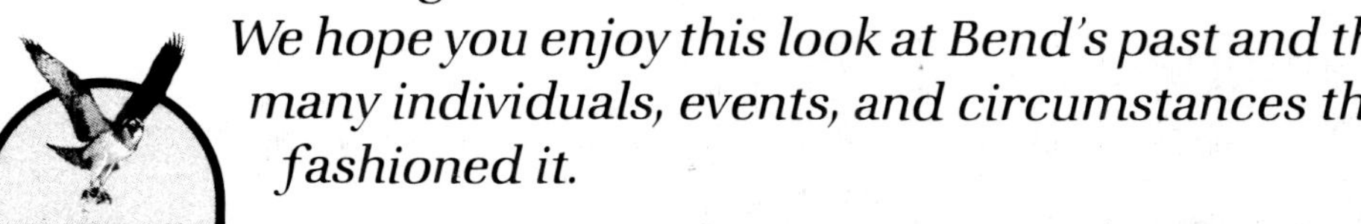

We hope you enjoy this look at Bend's past and the many individuals, events, and circumstances that fashioned it.

Bend sent this beautiful flower float to Portland's rose festival in June 1946. The Water Pageant queen is in the wreath of flowers. Under the sign is a replica of the snow-capped Three Sisters, calling attention to Bend as a vacation land. The other young women are Water Pageant princesses representing the different sports to be enjoyed in the Bend Country. William Van Allen photo

a pictorial history of

THE BEND COUNTRY

by Elsie Horn Williams

acknowledgments

The following good friends, and personnel public and private, have been unstinting in their time in helping me to locate the many photographs and stories used in this book.

James Arbow; Carol Boyd; Charles Boyd, Mrs. Phil Brogan; Central Oregon Community College; Bend Chamber of Commerce; Thomas Del Rio; Deschutes County Historical Society; Deschutes Free Public Library; Virginia Colver Elliott; Robert Folley; Madge Smith Glassow; Deschutes Forest Service; Violet Mayne Franks; Mae McNaught Gladish; Joyce Tifft Gribskov, author of *Pioneer Spirits of Bend;* Claude Kelley; Gladys Mayne McFall; Gordon McKay for the Clyde McKay collection; Mary Merrill, for Operation Santa Claus; Oregon Desert Museum; Oregon Game Commission; Oregon Historical Society; Oregon State Highway Department; Petersen Rock Garden; Elsie Williams Roe; Romain Village; Cora Sather; Margaret Van Metre Smith; Marjorie Smith; Seven Mountains; Sunriver Properties; Rose Hunnel Steidl; Marjorie Hoover Tromblee; Mrs. William Van Allen and her grandson, William Thompson; Dorothy Vandevert; Eddie Williamson.

Today old Reid School once again serves Bend country residents since it has become the Deschutes County Museum. Members of the Deschutes County Historical Society are on hand to answer questions and to set up new displays as attics are emptied of articles that were freighted in from Shaniko, brought to the Oregon country in covered wagons, or were shipped in on an early train.

One room is set aside for the tools used to cut down trees that were made into lumber. There is a kitchen that great-great-grandma could step into and start making butter. There are pictures of grandpa, sitting stiff, driving the family car. Dad is in his first car with the

For information, write:
The Donning Company/Publishers
5659 Virginia Beach Boulevard
Norfolk, Virginia 23502

This is a special edition and is not for sale in bookstores or other retail outlets.

Printed in the United States of America

rumbleseat for offspring to giggle over, for Bend is a town where families continue to stay, up to the fifth and sixth generations, and that takes them back to when Bend was only a bend in the river.

This is a museum of the Bend country, not some distant past. Pioneers still living remember that man driving the six-horse team, pulling a freight wagon loaded with a turbine for a power plant that will give Bend its first electric lights. They have stories to tell the schoolchildren who flock through the museum with a teacher in tow.

The museum is not only filled with things, it is filled with memories. Courtesy of John Frye

contents

This gnarled old juniper tree has been growing beside Mirror Lake for hundreds of years before the dam below Newport Beidge turned the bend in the river into a lake. Like people, age has given it a strange type of beauty. Constant trimming of dead limbs has kept it growing up instead of squat like most junipers. Photo by William Van Allen; courtesy of the William Thompson collection

preface

"The Bend in the River" is what the explorers, immigrants, cattlemen, and gold seekers called this place on the Deschutes. Here they stopped to drink the icy cold water and to allow their stock to browse on the green grass. Many just passing through vowed to return. "Farewell Bend," they said when they reluctantly left to continue their journey.

The high Bend country remained isolated long after the rest of Oregon was fairly well settled. There are no records of any white men penetrating the Bend area, almost in the center of Oregon, before 1825. But Bend has grown quickly since the first cattlemen brought their herds of cattle across the Cascade Mountains from the Willamette Valley, and south from Tyeh Valley. Its past has been exciting. Many years have been crowded with historical importance and change.

Many special events are remembered by Bend residents, such as when Bend became incorporated, when the trains came, not one, but two, and when the big mills were built, also in pairs. Bend remembers the wars, beginning with World War I, the changes leading up to the wars, and subsequent ramifications of them. Finally, "Happy days are here again."

This is a pictorial history that we who are living today can pass on to those who will come after us. This is a record of history in the making. Many of those earliest settlers, and up to the fifth and sixth generations of those settlers, chose to live in Bend country because it is a nice place to live.

I wish I had space to name everyone who has been helpful in compiling this book, but the list is too long and I dare not leave anyone out. I am sorry I was unable to contact many old friends. Some were temporarily out of town, had moved away, or were otherwise unavailable. It is surprising how busy senior citizens can be in Bend. Some had only memories of parents, for cameras were few in the early days, and there were no professional photographers yet.

A special thanks to those who let me look through their boxes and albums of pictures and keepsakes, and an extra thanks for the interesting stories that, unfortunately, have had to be boiled down to short captions. There is a story behind every picture and caption to feed the imagination of the young and to bring up pleasant memories of their elders, who in the future will be considered among the ancestral pioneers. Where credit for photographs has not been given, it is either unknown, after being in my own collection for many years; it was taken by my mother, Susan Horn, with her square Brownie camera; or it was taken by me with my own Instamatic.

This is a nice view across the Deschutes River from the residential area west of the river. The Pilot Butte Inn, an old landmark, is no more. It was torn down and replaced with a new, modern telephone building. Newport Bridge is the third bridge to cross the river at Bend after the old Sizemore bridge, seldom used and remembered only by a few old-timers. The Tumalo Bridge, also upriver, was Bend's only bridge for people living across the river until the more convenient Newport was buit in 1913. Photo by William Van Allen; courtesy of the William Thompson collection

introduction

For the first time, under one cover, in this volume, are assembled in chronological order the history of the Bend country in over three hundred photographs, many of them never before reprinted.

The Bend country was a rugged, isolated area almost in the center of the state of Oregon, when seen by the first white explorers. For that reason, it was almost the last to be discovered by white men who followed Indian trails, led by Indian guides. It has a short, exciting history covering less than a century and a half from the first explorer to the present time.

Descendants of the first lost wagon train to stop at the bend in the river, where the town of Bend is now located, are still living here. There were no cameras to catch the likenesses of these people, so we can only tell their stories as remembered by their offspring.

Seeing or hearing about the lush meadows, cattlemen brought their herds, built log cabins, and drove or sent their cattle to market over a 1000-mile route that still has no roads. Their cabins were old when finally the few remaining were photographed.

A fire in the Deschutes County courthouse destroyed many early records. Another fire about the same time destroyed duplicate records in the state capital building. It was suspected that someone did a good job of covering up records he didn't want seen. So this history is doubly important while there are people still living who remember those early settlers and have grown up with the country and the town of Bend. Many people came to the country and left, leaving only their likenesses in group photographs, their names forgotten. When a last name is remembered, first names are often hazy or never known, for many were called only by a last name. And women were called "Mrs." even by close friends. A few later records have been kept by attorneys in the area.

Bend, itself, is a comparatively new town, having been organized with duly elected officers in 1904. Deschutes County was the last county to be formed in the state of Oregon, in 1916. Situated on the edge of the most extensive virgin yellow pine forest in the world, Bend waited for a railroad and the sawmills that would follow. It was a boom town that did not die or become a ghost town when the big mills cut their timber and shut down.

Bend is a living, thriving town that is not doubling and trebling its population as it did earlier in the century, but it is growing. Its scenery was discovered by Hollywood and skiiers practicing for the Olympics. The National Aeronautics and Space Administration discovered Bend country when they were preparing to send the first men to the moon. Senior citizens have discovered Bend is kind to its older people, and new nonpolluting industries are finding a hearty welcome in the Bend country.

We hope you will find many pleasant hours reviewing Bend's history in *Bend: A Pictorial History.*

With three beautiful bridges crossing the Deschutes River in the city of Bend, there is no longer any need to ford it at the old immigrant crossing at Farewell Bend (the present Pioneer Park in Bend). This log bridge is at the location of the first Tumalo Bridge. It was called the Tumalo Bridge because it was on the only road to Tumalo Creek and was the only bridge inside the city limits to cross over to the west side of the river. The first Tumalo Bridge was also made from peeled logs but was not as attractively put together. Bend does not have a lot of snow, but when it does snow Bend people grab their cameras to take pictures.

Bend's other two bridges cross the Deschutes further down. About a mile north of Tumalo Bridge, Newport Bridge crosses the Bend Water and Light Power dam that formed Mirror Pond. Half a mile further down the river to the north, Portland Bridge, the last to be built, overlooks Pioneer Park. There the early travelers rested in a pleasant meadow before fording the river and said, "Farewell, Bend," before continuing on to wherever they were going. Courtesy of the Oregon State Highway Department

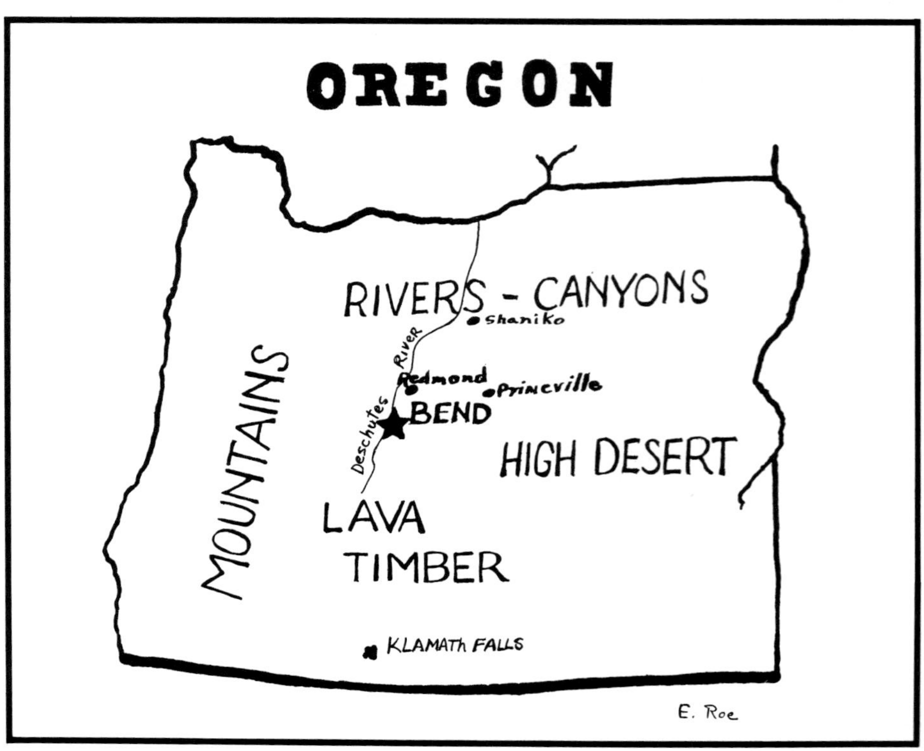

This map shows isolated Bend between high mountains, deep river canyons, and a desert. Map drawn by Elsie Williams Roe

Early travelers going to or through the Bend country were told to watch for Smith Rock, rising above the tableland over the three river canyons. It was one of the few places a man could climb down into a canyon to reach the Crooked River. Immigrants were warned that they must stay south of the Rocks as they traveled west. This route took them to the bend in the Deschutes River where they could drink their fill after many miles with no fresh water. Then they could follow the Deschutes south to Diamond Peak and the lower Willamette Valley and points south or west. If there were no wagons and only horseback riders, they could ford the Deschutes and follow the Indian trail north through Warm Springs Reservation to the Barlow Toll Road where they would join the Oregon Trail to the upper Willamette communities. In late fall, they might follow Williamson's and Sheridan's railroad survey across to the Santiam River midway between the other two passes.

Upriver from Smith Rock, several miles east, Crooked River Canyon widens into a small meadow. Here Barney Prine established his early-day way station for miners stopping for the night and refreshments on their way to the gold fields in eastern Oregon. Prineville became a prosperous cow town and the county seat of Crook County in 1893, taking land from the south half of Wasco County.

It was a steep climb up the south side of the Crooked River Canyon to reach the top where Pilot Butte would guide the travelers the rest of the way to Farewell Bend.

An infrequent blanket of snow covers one of the many cinder cones south-southeast of Bend. This area was one of the most extensive yellow pine forests in the world before the big mills started cutting their timber. In August 1907, Congress put an agricultural appropriations bill on President Theodore Roosevelt's desk for his signature. The amendment prohibited the creation of any more forest reserves in six western states without the consent of Congress. The President was not sure all twenty-one forest reserves he created before signing the bill were necessary, but it was better to be safe than sorry. One of them was the Deschutes National Forest in Central Oregon near Bend. Courtesy of the Oregon Forest Service

Wickiup Reservoir covers Wickiup Prairie, named for the teepee or wickiup poles left standing on an Indian trail between Klamath Lake in Southern Oregon and the Columbia River. This was a regular stopping place for the Klamath Indians on their way north. Even in bad weather, the wickiups, wrapped in their tule mats, became warm shelters, and the horses could rest and browse on the lush grass.

The Indians would reach the Columbia in time for the salmon run. Men would fish off high platforms over the river, and race their horses and gamble with other tribes that gathered at Celilo Falls during the fishing season. The women smoked the fish and got caught up with the news. On their way back south they picked huckleberries and stopped again on Wickiup Prairie, keeping to the west side of the Deschutes River until they reached the Little Deschutes. From the author's collection

The photograph shows the deceptively deep and turbulent Deschutes River a few miles south of Bend at the island. From the author's collection

The Deschutes River above Bend is almost a continuous waterfall. Two of the longest cascades are Dillon and Benham Falls. From the author's collection

It was called Red Butte on many early maps, on account of its red cinders that showed up at a great distance. It was called Pilot Butte by travelers who looked for the high, prominent landmark that would lead them to the bend in the river. It was not hard to tell Pilot Butte from the rash of smaller cinder cones scattered on the desert and in the woods to the south. The road leading to the butte later became Greenwood Avenue. It was long used by early travelers before the automobile was invented. Courtesy of Clyde McKay collection

The Three Sisters and Broken Top dominate the western sky in the Bend country. A heavy growth of pine forest covers the foreground. From the author's collection

Mount Jefferson, a perfect cone, never loses its snowcap in the summer. In the Mount Jefferson wilderness area, where wheeled vehicles are not allowed, one needs to backpack to get near it. Plainly visible from the highway and from Bend, north of the Three Sisters, it towers 10,497 feet in the sky and looks almost close enough to touch in the rarefied air.

Yellow pines like those in the foreground will be allowed to live their life spans without sign of a saw. From the author's collection

Spectacular Castle Cliffs overlooks East Lake high on Paulina Mountain. It is often called Lake of Mystery because the water remains clear and fresh with no visible inlet or outlet. Geologists believe that when Mount Newberry collapsed, forming Newberry Crater, the huge bowl held only one lake, higher than Crater Lake. Later upthrusts within the crater divided it into three lakes. East Lake was one of them. From the author's collection

Paulina Lake, another of the three lakes in Newberry Crater. Courtesy of Madge Smith Glassow collection

This is Drake Park where Bend began, where the first log cabin was built. It is where bands play, where artists hold their fairs, and where ducks race to greet visitors offering food. There are park benches and tables where a family can spread a lunch, or just spend a pleasant hour under the trees and watch the Deschutes River flow by. There are eleven acres of trees and lawn where once was meadow grass, only a block from the center of the original town of Bend. Courtesy of William Van Allen collection

I

1825-1877

It never seems right to start history when white men first come into a country, but where do we start when natives were passing through the country for generations? The Klamaths were only passing through the Bend country on their way to the fishing grounds on the Columbia River. They didn't stay.

The first explorers, Peter Skene Ogden and others who came after this Hudson's Bay party looking for beaver grounds, didn't stay or return. They came while Andrew Jackson was president.

The Warm Springs Indians who were so helpful in guiding these early explorers through the Bend country were unaware that they would be told to share their land with enemy tribes and that land would be called a reservation. White men found their Warm Springs homeland unacceptable for farming, or they, too, might have been moved elsewhere.

So we start history with those first explorers and the lost wagon trains of immigrants who had not found the road they had expected to find when they left the wagon train at Snake River. Somehow, those early roadbuilders had found that roadbuilding into the Bend country was too hard. Those early wagon trains would have to find their own way into the Willamette valley. None of those early immigrants returned, but some of their offspring did.

Chief Paulina and his warriors had gone on a warpath when white men wanted their land, and the peace-loving Chief Joseph was leading the old men, women, and children to safety in Canada when one of the first wireless telegraph messages told the army where they could be found. Caught just before crossing the line into Canada, they were taken to a bleak reservation in Indian Territory where many of the chief's followers would perish, never to see their beloved Walla Walla Mountains again. White men had found gold in their mountains.

Peter Skene Ogden and his party were probably the first white men to enter the Bend country. It was the largest party ever to enter the Snake country area where Ogden was the new chief trader for the Hudson's Bay Company. The party consisted of twenty-five lodges, two gentlemen, two interpreters, and seventy-one men with eighty guns, 364 beaver traps, 372 horses, and possibly Ogden's Indian wife.

Histories are not clear how this large party entered the Bend country that cold December in 1824. One rather suspects they followed up the Deschutes River on the west side instead of attempting a crossing where it gushed down into the Columbia River. They went down into the canyon where the Indians had almost spanned the canyon with their fishing scaffolds and had built a flimsy bridge from one side to the other intended only for foot traffic.

Seeing level ground with sparse sagebrush, Ogden attempted a crossing, breaking down the bridge and losing three of his horses. This is probably where he split his party, those who hadn't crossed following up the Deschutes and then around the head of the Metolius River until they reached the Indian crossing. This might have been where he lost forty-three men by desertion or having them join independent American trappers who were paying more for beaver fur.

Ogden would not have found a way to cross the deep Deschutes and Crooked River canyons for several miles east above the Crooked River. Then he would have to have followed the Crooked River back almost to the Deschutes if he reached the park later named for him. Courtesy of the Oregon Historical Society

Not waiting for Ogden to return next fall, Dr. John McLoughlin, chief factor for Hudson's Bay Company's Western Division, sent Archibald McDonald and Thomas McKay to look for Ogden and to do some trapping on their own. Ogden surprised McLoughlin by arriving down the Willamette Valley, having crossed the Cascade Mountains over some southern pass.

McLoughlin ordered all beaver dams in the Snake Country destroyed, hoping this would discourage the immigration of farmers who would spoil the fur trade. The expected lakes and small streams were dried up and wagon trains that had taken this cut-off route to the Willamette Valley suffered great hardships.

In August 1827, Ogden was off again, hoping to catch up to McDonald's party that had crossed the divide between the Deschutes and Klamath River basins. Ogden reported they had found an abundance of desert and the greatest number of Indians in North America, but little game and few furs. Courtesy of the Oregon Historical Society

Nathaniel Wyeth came next through the Bend country, in the winter of 1834 and 1835, looking for beaver and leaving no sign that he had passed through. He had grandiose ideas about making a fortune exporting beaver pelts and salt salmon that he would send around Cape Horn in his own ships. The salmon run was poor that year and his ship was late—his property, including Fort Hall, on the Snake River, and his holdings on Sauvies Island, in the Columbia River, went to Hudson's Bay Company by default. He went back to the East, never to return to the Bend country. Courtesy of the Oregon Historical Society

The Thomas Clark immigrant wagon train was the first one known to stop at the Bend in the River, possibly where Pioneer Park is now. That fall of 1851, Grace Clark, Tom's nineteen-year-old sister, had been almost scalped and needed time to recuperate after their long trek from the Snake River. Their mother and brother had been shot and scalped soon after they left the Oregon Trail to take a shorter route over a road that was supposed to have been made across the Willamette Pass.

Finding no roadbuilders' blaze marks, they crossed the Deschutes to follow an old Indian trail north to reach Barlow Toll Road. Many in that party must have looked back on the pleasant meadow and cool water to say, "Farewell, Bend," not knowing what hazards they would find ahead. Grace Clark did not return, but her sons must have heard her talk about that place on the river because they were among the Bend country's earliest pioneers.

The now-famous lost Elliot wagon train was next to find the Bend in the River, mistaking one of the Three Sisters for Diamond Peak further south. Almost 250 wagons and 1,027 people waited beside the river in 1853, while scouts looked for the blazed trees that would lead them across the mountains to upper Willamette Valley.

This is the bend in the river where the lost wagon train stoppd to rest and to search out the road that was to be built across the mountains. It is where they said "Farewell Bend," as they reluctantly continued on to meet friends and relatives on the other side of the Cascades. The name "Farewell Bend" became the first name of the small community that later dropped the "Farewell" and became simply "Bend." From the author's collection

Dr. John Strong Newberry was with the Abbot party in 1855. He was the first to describe the Paulina area, and it is for him that the Newberry Crater was finally named. It is doubtful that he saw all the wonders of this area or realized the height of 7,985-foot Paulina Peak, remnant of the dome of a vanishing mountain summit overlooking the crater. These formation resulted from a geological upheaval that took place less than 10,000 years ago. Courtesy of the U.S. Forest Service

The history of the Paulina area is told and felt (with a shaking of the floor under the visitor's feet) at the Lava Lands Visitor's Center, eleven miles south of Bend, at the foot of Lava Butte. Trails that lead to points of interest are preserved by the Forest Service.

Many lava casts remain in what was once a forest of large trees before the eruption of the volcano. Although the trees were burned out, cooling lava preserved their forms. Philip Brogan, a former editor of the *Bend Bulletin*, is a self-taught geologist and anthropologist who has written many articles and a book about the lava cast area. Courtesy of the U.S. Forest Service

The Williamson-Abbot railroad surveying party came into the Bend area from California in 1855. They followed the Little Deschutes River until it joined the Deschutes River coming from the mountains in the west. A short distance further, on, the river spread out on a low prairie. Here, the two leaders separated, each with a military escort. Abbot went north and Williamson went west to Crane Prairie.

Lieutenant Henry Larcom Abbot's party continued north, following the river until they had to go around a tall cinder cone that had spewed lava down into the river, diverting it from its original course.

Abbot wrote in his diary that he met several groups of men who were searching for a creek where two little girls had found some gold nuggets and had put them in their little blue buckets. The children had been with a lost immigrant train and no one knew where the nuggets had been picked up. Men are still looking for the Blue Bucket Mine.

Abbot later had a brilliant career in the Army Corps of Engineers during the Civil War. He was also a member of the board of consulting engineers that was named by President Theodore Roosevelt to prepare plans for the construction of the Panama Canal. And he was also remembered when a camp for engineers was built in the Bend country during World War II. Courtesy of Oregon Historical Society; on loan from the William Van Allen collection

Lieutenant Robert Stockton Williamson and his party, including Lieutenant Philip "Little Phil" Sheridan and Lieutenant George Crook's military attachment, went west of Abbot's route to Crane Prairie in 1855. Courtesy of the Oregon Historical Society; on loan from the William Van Allen collection

Lieutenant George Crook and Lieutenant Philip Sheridan were back in the Bend country during the Piute Indian uprising against the white settlers. Sheridan made camp with his detachment of soldiers in a grove of yellow pines west of the future town of Sister and south of the McKenzie Highway. A sign points to Whispering Pines Campground where Sheridan carved his name and the date on the largest tree. The tree measures twenty feet and two inches in circumference as high as a man could reach. Other trees still standing surrounding the Sheridan tree measure fourteen feet to twenty-two feet in circumference. This grove was set aside as a primitive area. Crook, raised to a major-general, was honored later when Crook County was cut out of Wasco County. Crook is remembered by many people for sneaking up on a small Indian camp and killing many Indians without asking whether or not they had any connection with the wily Chief Paulina he was seeking. From the author's collection

Dr. William McKay, pictured here, served in Lieutenant-Colonel George Crook's 1866 to 1867 campaign against Chief Paulina's Snake Indians. McKay led the Warm Springs scouts that participated in that long search for the wily Chief Paulina. McKay was the grandson of the Indian wife of Hudson's Bay's chief factor, Dr. John McLoughlin. His good medical education was paid for by McLoughlin. Photograph from a wet-plate photo; courtesy of the Oregon Historical Society

Seated in this photograph is Dr. William McKay's brother, Donald, one of the Warm Springs scouts who helped to run down Captain Jack during the war with the Modoc Indians. Standing is Dr. McKay. The boy is William's son. Donald exploited his part in the Modoc War by traveling with a medicine show, dispensing his famous cure-all Indian medicines that contained mostly alcohol, sugar, and aloes. Courtesy of the Oregon Historical Society

Indian Head Rock, on the Warm Springs Reservation, is north of Kah-nee-ta Resort, which furnishes teepees, cabins, campground, and two warm swimming pools for guests. The Warm Springs Indians are on their way to becoming independently rich with their resort, sawmill, and other enterprises. Like their neighbors in Bend, they are always ready to join in a parade. From the author's collection

This shows the Deschutes River at Cline Falls, twenty miles north of Bend, in the Redmond area. Cline Falls was named for a dentist who filed on a claim at the falls in 1888. He commuted on horseback from his homestead to take care of his Prineville practice, traveling a distance equivalent to twenty-four miles by modern highway. Courtesy of Madge Smith Glassow collection

II

1877-1900

Covered wagon trains had been pouring into the Willamette valley for a quarter of a century. Tall silk hats had replaced beaver hats, since the days of the fur traders were long past, and the Indians had been subdued when the first cattlemen brought their cattle across the Cascades to fatten on the rich meadow grass in the Bend country.

President Ulysses S. Grant was in his first year of office, Portland would reach a population of 18,000 by 1880, and Abigail Scott Duniway would be sung down in church for talking out for women's rights. But there were no white women's voices in the Bend country. Wives were waiting for the country to become "civilized."

Indian women, on their way between their Klamath Indian Reservation and their fishing grounds on the Columbia River, stopped to peddle their woven sweetgrass baskets and wild huckle--berries they had picked along the way.

Prineville, the nearest town, had survived the first rush of gold seekers passing through to the gold fields in eastern Oregon and Idaho and had settled down to being a quiet cow town. Bend's early cattlemen were anxious for a change and vied with each other in inducing newcomers to settle nearby to form a nucleus of a new and thriving town.

In 1877, Cort Allen and W. H. Staats paced off their adjoining homesteads on the bend in the river just south of the immigrants' river crossing, and thought they had built their cabins within their lines. A later government survey found both cabins on Staats's property. Allen moved his stock up to Big Meadows, where Sunriver Resort is now.

The Allen cabin was used at various times by trappers, as a storage place for pack rats, for a Sunday school, and for an infrequent church service. It was also used for a school and a newspaper office before being moved to Drake Park where it was hoped it would be preserved. It finally fell apart and had to be destroyed. Courtesy of Clyde McKay collection

This old W. P. Vandevert homestead house was an addition to the Sisemore or Todd log cabin just above the Big Meadow. Old Bill, son of Grace Clark Vandevert, returned to the Bend country with his family in 1891. His wife was a schoolteacher from Kentucky. Bill, his wife, two daughters, Mittye and Maude, and two sons, Clint and George, first went to live with Bill's remarried father, who had a homestead in the Powell Butte area. Here, Bill's son Claude was born. Claude lived at the old homestead, south of Bend, and ran the ranch until his death in 1975 at age 83. Arthur and Grace, the last of the Vandevert children, were born on the old homestead. The homestead was adjacent to their uncles' (Dick, Walter, and Charles Vandevert) spreads near the present Sunriver Lodge.

Old Bill liked to tell about camping between the river and the site of the future famous Pilot Butte Inn. He also liked to tell about riding horseback from Powell Butte to the old homestead. Courtesy of Dorothy Vandevert collection

The Vandevert men get their winter's meat. Old Bill is on the left. Jack Vandevert, widower of Grace Clark Vandevert, is seated. The date of the photograph is unknown. Courtesy of Dorothy Vandevert collection

Claude Vandevert stands with his dogs in the backyard of the old homestead. Claude was the grandson of Grace Clark Vandevert. Courtesy of Dorothy Vandevert collection

The Vandevert children went to school at Rosland (La Pine), south of Bend. Their teacher was Carrie Fee. Students were often as old as the teacher or even older. Carrie Fe is standing behind Mittye, who is seated. Grace Vandevert has her arm on Mittye's lap. Clint Vandevert is the tallest boy; George is also holding his hat. The smallest boy is Claude Vandevert. The other children probably are Fees. Courtesy of Dorothy Vandevert

The remains of the early Swalley dam and small sawmill that cut only flume lumber were still visible when this picture was taken in the early 1900s. The Swalleys, mother and sons, dug many miles of ditches under the Cary Act before leaving the country.

The old Steidl and Tweet Dam can be seen from the highway as one enters Bend from the north. The dam raised the water so it would flow into the flume without being pumped. From the author's collection

III

1900-1904

The Bend country had been cattle country until Alexander Drake showed up with ideas of irrigating the dry land after the Carey Act was passed by Congress in 1897. Others came, building dams and digging irrigation ditches.

There were other men from the Midwest, who had seen the end of the great pine forests in Minnesota, the Dakotas, and Michigan. They knew the rich timber barons would find some way to reach Central Oregon's yellow pines—the best land had already been bought with railroad scrip from the government for a few dollars an acre. While the timber lasted, they knew Bend would be a boom town, and then it would die as so many Midwest towns had done. They took up timber claims as near as possible to the big timber claims and waited.

S. A. D. Puter had been a timber cruiser for a gang of timber thieves on the west side of the Cascades, and he saw his chance to get rich on a big stand of timber a few miles southeast of Bend that the big lumber companies had overlooked. He staged something like the Oklahoma Rush, except this time it was for cheap timber. It was a good plan, if only a certain newly-appointed, goateed forest ranger had not been watching. The Oregon Land Fraud Cases made headline news for several years.

People around Bend read the newspapers avidly, then passed them around until they were dog-eared, not safe to use out back. Puter talked and men in high government places were implicated. A United States senator from Oregon was found guilty of receiving money under his desk. He died from having a tooth pulled before he went to jail. A Portland attorney, a state representative from the Bend district, and the Secretary of the Interior from Portland were indicted—men the people had known and had voted for.

President McKinley was shot and the vice-president, Theodore (Teddy) Roosevelt assumed office. A conservationist, he began feeding Congress bills to stop the giveaway of government timber.

At Christmas, 1901, W. H. Staats, Postmaster, and L. D. Wiest decided Bend should have a yuletime party and that everyone should be invited. Everybody came, all seven households. The party was held in the Pilot Butte Inn dining room. A tall tree was brought in from Tumalo Creek, probably a stray hemlock or fir. The ladies were delegated to trim the tree, no doubt with paper chains and lighted candles. It was loaded with gifts, unwrapped. Gifts were never wrapped but added to the decorations when paper was scarce. Wiest acted as Santa Claus and no one minded going home in the snow when it was over. Ovid Riley, a bachelor, lived on his ranch six miles down the river. Charles J. Cottor went in the same direction just north of the present Pioneer park. The Wiests lived on their homestead, now occupied by a Chevron station on northeast Third Street. John Sisemore passed Staats's log cabin less than a mile. The Drake's house (they called it a hunting lodge), was on the future Mirror Pond. The site is now occupied by a free parking lot. Mr. and Mrs. Brock managed the Pilot Butte Inn.

Trail Crossing Road was blasted out of the side of Crooked River Canyon downriver from the Cow Canyon road. It was steeper, with many more dangerous sharp curves than Cow Canyon, but it bypassed Prineville and brought Shaniko many miles closer. Even after many letters of protest, mail continued to go around by Prineville to be sorted there, delaying the delivery of letters, packages, and newspapers by several days. Not until Bend had a railroad was the routing changed.

Freighters couldn't believe what they saw when Dad West started plowing up streets for Drake's new town of Bend. People out north of Drake's town were told a railroad terminal would be built in their area, and they immediately platted the town of Lytle, naming it after the bearer of the good news. Staats had already decided that his Deschutes would be the coming town, but freighters were finding the new Pilot Butte Inn closer to the road between Shaniko and Silver Lake, with better cooks. Max Luddemann started the *Bend Bulletin* from the Allen log cabin, and the school had been moved to the one-room school building on a rock pile closer to the center of the population. (Bend had grown from 21 legal voters to 104). Women could not vote, but there were few women in the Bend country, and those who were had their hands full raising children and keeping the dust wiped away. Single teachers were sought after and were soon married to the men of their choice. They had little time to think of Abigail Duniway and her crusade for women's right to vote.

In 1900, the population in the Deschutes precinct of Crook County, an area of about eighteen by forty miles, was twenty-one. During the presidential election, the voters split their votes between McKinley and Teddy Roosevelt.

Alexander Drake's vacation house on a wagon, forerunner of the motor home, stopped on a high rocky ridge overlooking the Deschutes River. Mrs. Drake watched the sun go down behind the Three Sisters, turning the snow-covered peaks a rose pink. The river hurried around the bend, coming from the west at that point. No doubt a fish, or a half dozen, jumped for dragonflies. Diving ducks swam undisturbed under willow trees across the river; beyond was a backdrop of a dark pine forest. Mrs. Drake decided it was an ideal place to build a fishing lodge.

Alexander Drake, in his mind's eye, was building dams to harness the fast-flowing stream to water thousands of acres of dry land under a new reclamation project that had been passed in 1897 as the Cary Act. Drake had gone first to look over the dry land in Arizona where he met Charles Cottor, who had been to the Deschutes country.

With Cottor as fishing guide, they unobtrusively searched out good dam sites. The next year, the Drakes were back, hiring "Dad" West (Douglas Ward's grandfather) to build their hunting lodge, a showplace in the wilderness. Courtesy of the *Pioneers' Gazette*, January 1981

The Steidl and Tweet sawmill, built north of Pioneer Park, was later sold to Henry Linster.

It was above this bend in the river that the Clark immigrant wagon train stopped for Grace to recuperate from her near-scalping. A bronze plaque was placed here but has since been stolen, presumably for the copper. From the author's collection

Alexander Drake's Pilot Butte Development Company canal took water from the Deschutes River three miles above Bend, opposite a tiny brush-covered island. The canal would furnish water for Bend's population of 226. The Weist homestead on the future East Third Street was the first to receive water from this flume in 1905. Lateral flumes served other residences. In 1911 a pressure system put water in a high wooden tank on top of Water Tower Hill, later changed to Hospital Hill when the Saint Charles Hospital was built on the hill. The water flowed down into the residences and business establishments by gravity.

Drake sold this system to the Oregon Irrigation Company. When he sold the rest of his holdings he stipulated that this would be the only ditch taking water out of the river above Bend. Photograph by Susan Horn

Here a canal is under construction. This is a main artery. Smaller ditches will take water out of it through flume gates that measure the water going to each ranch. A ditch rider will check for leaks in the main canal and will adjust the gates to see that the ranches receive the amount of water paid for. Ranchers paid for their water rights according to the number of acres they wanted to irrigate. This photograph shows how the sides of the canals were built up, rather than digging the ditch down into the ground. This is to keep the water flowing downhill over the uneven ground. From the author's collection

Flumes often carried water for miles to bridge low land to reach ranches on higher ground. Some of the small sawmills cut nothing but flume lumber. Graft was rampant during the early years after the Cary Act was passed. Many pioneers remember when only a couple of men were hired to dig ditches with picks and shovels, then were not paid for their work by their unscrupulous employers who left the country as soon as they collected their money from the government. From the author's collection

On the back of this photograph, in fine writing, is this notation: "The old bridge across the Deschutes just above Tumalo, about 1905 or 6."

Claude Kelley says this is not the Sisemore toll-free bridge he fished from as a boy. Gordon McKay says he recognized the terrain, and that it is that bridge. It is doubtful if any other old-timer is around to furnish positive proof of just where this bridge was located. The author agrees with Gordon. The railing was added later, changing the looks of the bridge. Courtesy of Madge Smith Glassow collection

Drake's first sawmill was built upriver from the Farewell Bend Ranch. Sisemore's bridge can be seen downriver in the distance. This was the first free bridge across the Deschutes, costing $2,000 to build. As the Deschutes District Road Supervisor for Crook County, Sisemore managed to have a poll tax help pay for the bridge. From the author's collection

Drake's Pilot Butte Inn was a sudden success and put a stop to the Sisemore-Staats feud over attracting customers to their respective hotels. Staats had begun serving fresh vegetables to his guests after his handmade water wheel brought water up from the Deschutes River to water his garden. Sisemore's toll-free bridge across the river from his Farewell Bend Hotel didn't entice many customers away from Staats's more conveniently located hostelry, since not many people had reasons for crossing the river.

Drake's new Pilot Butte Inn, built in 1902, was even closer to the watering place on the river and caught the traffic coming in on Wall Street from any direction. Also, the Keever women that Drake brought in from Prineville were excellent cooks. Gathered on the porch of the inn that fronts on Wall Stret are the Keever women and Fred and Ralph Lucus, sons of the new owner, Ralph Lucus, Sr. Courtesy of Marjorie Smith collection

This picture answers the questions, "Where was the first Pilot Butte Inn, and what happened to it?" After Ralph Lucus bought the original inn in 1904, he built an addition onto the front, bringing it closer to Wall Street. This left the dining room and the upstairs with the diamond-shaped window facing north. In 1910 Greenwood was no more than a narrow road coming onto Wall Street from the east facing the watering place in the river. When the last Pilot Butte was built and the streets widened, it left Greenwood facing the inn. Rather than put a jog in Greenwood, Newport Avenue crossed the Deschutes River when the new Newport Bridge was built, allowing the street to end on Wall Street. Courtesy of Marjorie Smith collection

This is the new bridge over Tumalo Creek about the place where the Indians crossed on their way from the Columbia River to Klamath Marsh. It was built in 1965. Courtesy of Claude Kelley collection

Bend's first schoolhouse, built with donated funds, was on the north end of the lava pile and a little lower than where the county courthouse now stands. It was painted white and had a bell tower. It was built in 1904 after the old log cabin on the Staats's homestead became too small. Almost at once, the new one-room schoolhouse was overflowing when ten new students arrived to fill only six empty desks. Students were again shifted to empty rooms in one business building after another. Taxpayers knew they had to do something.

There was a short period between Sisemore's Farewell Bend school and the new school on the lava bed when new settlers near the Staats's trading post area wanted the school moved closer. The old Allen log cabin was cleaned out and a few benches were made for the children to sit on. School-age students soon outgrew the old log cabin and some classes were held in various empty room in business buildings. Courtesy of the *Bend Bulletin* before the new school was built.

Antone Aune, Theodore Aune, and Theodore's son came to Bend from Minnesota in 1903 and built this white Aune Hotel and rooming house. The house is across the street from Bend Hardware. Minnesota Street had changed when this photo of a tourist on horseback with her donkeys was taken in 1910. She is heading west, after crossing Bond Street, coming by way of Lava Road.

The Bend Hardware, built by Dement, faces Bond Street. Courtesy of Clyde McKay collection; on loan from Gorden McKay

In 1903, Drake hired Nick Smith to build a rock wall from the Staats property to the Pilot Butte barn. Gradually, it was torn down to make room for new buildings. A 1910 photo shows the wall intact, leading to Franklin Street. The Johnson Building is the three-story building on the right. It had a number of different occupants through the years. Courtesy of Marjorie Smith collection

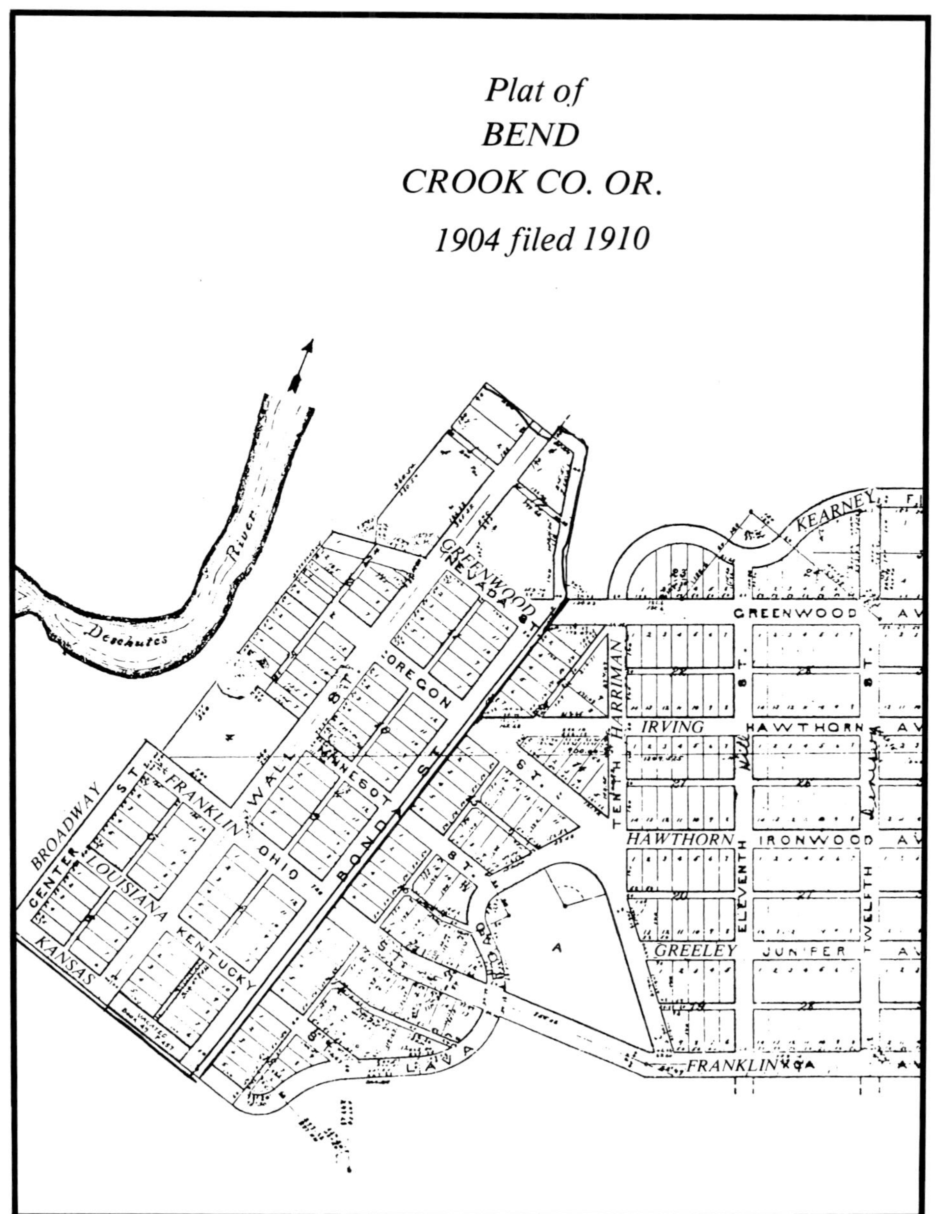

Ranchers couldn't believe their eyes when they saw "Dad" West plowing streets through good grazing land. When they asked West what it was all about he said it was for Drake's new town of Bend. Drake gave his streets all flowery names as well as names of trees and of famous people.

Others had different names for the streets that were more appropriate, although some of Drake's names are still used.

The street the Aune Hotel faced a couple of years later naturally became Minnesota Street. Drake had hired Nick Smith to build a rock wall along his property to keep out the livestock that stopped to graze in his year. The freighters that used the road that ran past the wall called the main street "Wall Street," as it continues to be called. Lawrence built his real estate building on Wall Street and what else but "Lawrence Street"? The first banks were on Bond Street. Bend had to have an Oregon Street, and the road that went across the bridge was Tumalo Road. The bridge became "Tumalo Bridge" even though Tumalo Creek was four miles away. Tumalo Road is now Century Drive, a scenic 100-mile drive past many mountain lakes and close to the foot of 9,000-foot Bachelor Butte.

Drake's original plat was discovered by Joyce Tifft Gribskov, author of *Pioneer Spirits of Bend*, and was graciously lent to this author. Courtesy of Joyce Tifft Gribskov

This post office was the first building on Wall Street. It was built in 1901 or 1902 and was made with rough lumber rather than logs. The photograph was taken several years later, after other buildings were built further north on Wall Street. The Thomas Tripletts lived in a tent south of the post office when they first came to Bend.

This was the third post office in the vicinity of Bend. Sisemore's was first, and Staats's was second. Courtesy of Claude Kelley collection

When a Mr. Lytle, an official of the Columbia Southern Railroad, told landowners north of Bend that his railroad would be continuing south from Shaniko and would need a terminal site, they immediately platted the city of Lytle.

Laidlaw, renamed Tumalo, had the Tumalo irrigation project from Tumalo Creek. With hopes of a railroad coming across the desert from Burns and bypassing Bend to cross the Cascades on the Abbot-Williamson survey, it was also a contender for central Oregon's leading city. Courtesy of Madge Smith Glassow collection

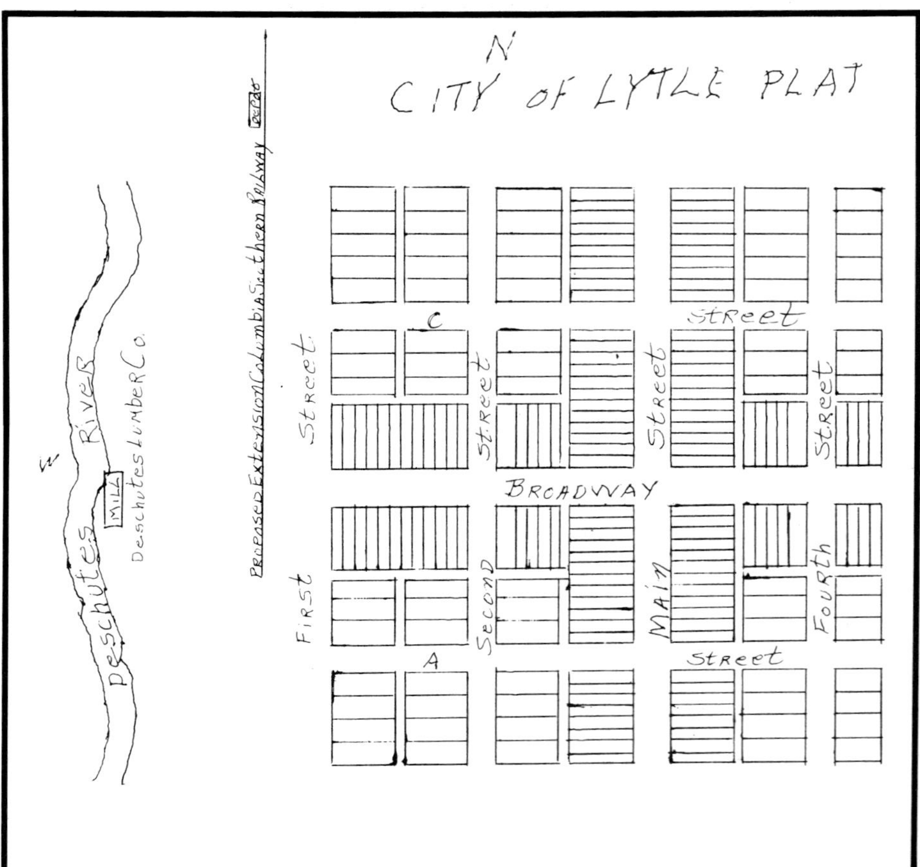

E. A. Sather bought the Pine Tree Building from Drake and started the first store on Wall Street in 1903. Mrs. Sather and her son, Ted, are shown here behind the store. The Sathers lived upstairs for several years before building their new home at the corner of Broadway and Kansas streets. The upstairs of the store was then used for a dance hall and for shows. The first "flickers" in Bend were shown there. The store became simply "Sather's" when all the pine trees were cut down on Wall Street by Frank Filey, who was hired to do the job. Courtesy of Cora Sather collection

The old Cort Allen log cabin had been used for a schoolhouse, Sunday school, and infrequently for church services before Max Luddemann set up his hand set press and started publishing the *Bend Bulletin* in 1903. The first issue of the four-page weekly newspaper printed the names of all eleven children attending school and their ages. The *Bulletin* also listed the names of the twenty-one voters and a count of their family members as an unofficial census report. Luddemann (with the hat) stands beside the door while his printer wears an apron. The other men have not been identified. The photograph, no doubt, was taken with Luddemann's camera.

The students mentioned, ranging from seven to sixteen years of age, were: Nellie Barnes; John Bates; Ralph and Fred Lucus; Prince Staats; Steve Steidl; May and Robert Triplett; and Iva, Margaret, and Pauline West. Courtesy of the *Bend Bulletin*

Monday, December 19, 1904 was a big day at Bend. Without giving up hopes of being the center of a new town, the 101 voters agreed that they needed a central government with a mayor, city councilmen, and minor officers. Most of all, they wanted a policeman to round up a few drunks that were beginning to drift in and send them on their way. Besides the two saloons, stretched within a few blocks of the river were two sawmills, three general stores, two butcher shops, and four hotels.

Before the election, posters with caricatures of the two leading candidates began to appear in store and office windows. There were rallies and speeches. Two men ran on every ticket to make the election interesting. F. H. Shonquest and Hugh O'Kane tossed dice to see which one would run for councilman. Shonquest won the toss and the election. There is no record of where the election was held, but it might well have been at the school in Allen's log cabin.

Bend's cornet band marched to the home of A. L. Goodwillie to serenade Bend's first mayor, who was also the postmaster. The defeated candidate, shouldering a shotgun and carrying pistols in two pockets, stalked the town, apparently in good fun, before leaving Bend. It was learned later that he was wanted by the law in a distant town.

Warren Glaze, seated in the photograph, was the band instructor for Bend's first band. He was born in Prineville sometime before 1862. Courtesy of Madge Smith Glassow collection

IV

1904-1911

The Oregon Land Fraud Cases were getting national attention. An Oregon United States senator had been found guilty of receiving money under the table. A cabinet member had been called home to Oregon to testify. A pretty land office worker was hiding out. "Teddy" Roosevelt ran again for president and was reelected. Abigail Scott Duniway was still stumping the state for women's suffrage.

The male voters in Deschutes precinct elected a mayor and a city council before they had decided where their city would be. New businesses were springing up on Drake's Wall Street, and something needed to be done about the saloons on Bond Street. Bend needed to be incorporated so the citizens could make laws and vote money for a new school and a cemetery. Bend was incorporated in 1907 and the first policeman was hired. The volunteer firemen elected their own fire chief. Two railroad companies started laying competing tracks up the Deschutes River Canyon and men argued on how they would get across the Crooked River Canyon, or if they would stop on its edge as the Columbia Southern had done. Thomas Shevlin came looking for a site for a sawmill and said it would be built as soon as Bend had a railroad.

One of the most important changes on the Bend scene was when Clyde McKay bought Drake's holdings for the Bend Company. Many people suspected McKay was representing a more important lumber company than a Bend company with a small sawmill (purchased from Drake) and flumes that brought water to Bend residents. Bend was building quickly, and three young men tried making hand-molded bricks on the road to the Tumalo.

The whole western sky seemed to be on fire in July 1910. Smoke clouded the sun, and ashes with live coals came out of the forests east and west of Bend and set dry pine needles to smoldering. Mills stopped burning slash and their smokestacks stopped belching smoke when mills shut down because the woods were like dry tinder, ready to burst into flames. Men walking on the street were drafted and sent to fight forest fires in Idaho, Washington, and Montana. Small fires started in the forests around Bend were quickly smothered with wet gunnysacks soaked in water barrels on wagons. Men patroled the woods on foot with shovels over their shoulders, ready to cover the smallest flame with piles of dry dirt. A drenching rain put an end to the fires, but this worst fire season in history left an unknown number of people dead and millions of acres of forest destroyed.

The High Desert was filling up fast, keeping the small sawmills busy cutting rough lumber for their small desert shacks. The Bend Hardware and Nick Smith's Hardware stores sold them black tar paper to nail on the outside of their houses to keep out the wind and dust. During the Spanish Influenza epidemic of 1918, many homesteaders who had not left before the war started died without help. Only after they were missed, maybe weeks later, was it discovered that a whole family had died. It was a mystery how these isolated people could catch the flu.

Land segregated for irrigation also filled up with new farmers. This land was paid for, as well as water rights for irrigation. How the jackrabbits flourished on the new shoots of green alfalfa! Women stood with shotguns, protecting their gardens, only to have every leaf disappear during the night. No fence was tight enough to keep them out. Coyotes waited for a new calf to be born. Like the homesteaders, many of these people starved out or moved to town to take jobs or start new businesses. Unlike the homesteaders, they had land and water rights to sell—the homesteaders had nothing. Many homesteaders liked to tell the same story about why they left. They said they lived on brown beans and dried apples until the beans were gone. Then they ate dried apples for breakfast, drank water for dinner, and swelled up for supper. Finally they ran out of water.

In 1903 the Panama Canal treaty was signed. That would mean that someday ships from the West Coast would not have to sail around the Horn to reach East Coast markets.

This Baptist church, built in 1904, was a community church serving the Protestants until 1916 when the Methodists built their own church. It became known as "the little brown church" to differentiate it from a later church. For a few years before building their church, the Methodists rented the Baptist church twice a month for their special services, although their children continued to attend the combined Sunday school classes. The whole community enjoyed the Christmas tree at the Baptist church. Christmas 1906 seems to have been a special time. A back room built onto the church was used for the free public library before it was moved to a back room in the bank building on the corner of Wall and Oregon streets. The small library room in the church later became the young people's room where they had their parties every Friday night.

The O'Neils lived in the house beyond the church shown in this photograph. (They were not the O'Neils who had a family of boys and who built the log cabin school on the Farewell Bend Ranch.) The O'Neils who lived near the church had married daughters who did not move with them when they came to Bend from Kansas. O'Neil was a Civil War veteran.

The Baptist church was built in a triangle dividing Oregon Street from Irving. It was painted white with a hitching rack in front and was in a prominent location that could be seen from Wall Street. From the author's collection

Not all early bend pioneers came by stage. This item from the *Bend Bulletin* lists arrivals in 1905. Babies were born at home, and some never lived beyond their first year. Courtesy of the Deschutes *Pioneers' Gazette*

CENTRAL OREGON CHRONICLES 1905

(From **The Bend Bulletin**)

BORN:

Jan. 2. 11½-pound son, to Ralph Sheldon, blacksmith.
Feb. 12. Son, to Mr. and Mrs. C. H. Carter.
Feb. 28. Second daughter, to Mr. and Mrs. Charles Brock, at Lytle.
Mar. 8. Daughter, to Mr. and Mrs. W. H. Courtney.
May 3. Daughter, to William P. Downing, Tumalo homestead.
July 3. Daughter, to Mr. and Mrs. John Benfield, near Sisters.
July 21. 10-pound son, to Mr. and Mrs. Clarence Parker.
July 25. Son, to Mr. and Mrs. Richard Garman.
Aug. 13. 11-pound girl, to Merril Van Tassel, Squaw Creek.
Aug. 16. Daughter, to Mr. and Mrs. Oliver H. Erickson.
Aug. 17. Daughter, to Mr. and Mrs. John H. Overturf.
Sept. 11. Daughter, to Mr. and Mrs. C. L. Johnson, three miles west of Laidlaw.
Sept. 22. 9½-pound son, to Mr. and Mrs. W. B. Wilson, at Portland.
Oct. 10. Daughter, to Mr. and Mrs. John McLeod, Hobbs station.
Dec. Daughter "born last week" (**Bend Bulletin,** Dec. 8), to Dr. C. S. Edwards of Prineville.
Dec. 6. 9-pound daughter, to G. J. Shobert, at his home.

DIED:

Jan. 2. Charles Overton, aged 3 mos., 26 days; son of Mr. and Mrs. James W. Overton. D. of whooping cough and complications at Deschutes.

Jan. 6. Frank Poindexter, 2 yrs., 8 mos.; son of Mr. and Mrs. Ora Poindexter. D. of whooping cough and complications at Bend.

Jan. 26. Millie Barnes, 10 mos.; daughter of E. T. and Annie Barnes. D. of pneumonia and meningitis near Bend.

This cluster of the Charles Boyd family homestead buildings has belonged to some member of the Boyd family since the house was built in 1905, a year after Boyd arrived in Bend and was intrigued with the potential water power for a slaughterhouse. He built the slaughterhouse on the back of the original six acres near the river, where the Riverhouse is now. Ice was brought in from Arnold ice cave and sometimes from Swalley's pond. Boyd kept his slaughterhouse, his butchershop, and local residences in ice from his icehouse until he built his refrigeration plant some years later.

These three buildings were moved back on the family property when the front part was sold for the Bend River Mall Boyd Center. The buildings here have been placed in their original arrangement. The small bunkhouse and icehouse are used for storage of family antiques and purchased antiques that a grandson, Charles Boyd, Jr., is restoring. Photograph by Charles Boyd

These are the wedding photographs of Miss Cora Bell Chapman and Nicholas Paul Smith, taken in 1905 at The Dalles, Oregon. The future Mrs. Smith came west by train with Mrs. Sather, who was also met at The Dalles and acted as witness for the young couple. Both couples came from Bemidgi, Minnesota, and probably knew about the vast timber holdings near Bend of the Bemidgi-based Shevlin-Hixon Lumber Company, so expected that Bend would be a boom town one day. Courtesy of Marjorie Smith collection

This big bus won national attention in 1905 when its manager, Don R. Rea, of Auto Lines, announced the machine would be making regular scheduled trips from Cross Keys to Bend, the first bus in the United States to run on schedule. Dewey Tyler would be driving the machine built by W. C. Gill, in Portland. They would take four days to make the trip, stopping along the way for passengers to take pictures. Cross Keys seems to have been as short-lived as the bus that got no farther than Shaniko before quitting. Cross Keys shows on a map of Oregon in 1900 by George F. Cram, Chicago. It was on Antelope Creek. One suspects it might have been at the end of the Columbia Southern Railroad before it reached Shaniko, because that town is not shown. The artist must not have been too well informed because he has Bend well west of the Deschutes River and north of Tumalo Creek. But then, in 1900 there was no Bend. He does have a Roseland, now LaPine, and a place called Lava about the location of Welcome Bend, that is not on the map.

A group of young Bend people was allowed to ride two miles on the new bus that went the rest of the way to Shaniko at ten miles an hour. They walked back to Bend after their two-mile ride.

Dr. U. C. Coe, Bend's first doctor, the only one at that time, is seated on the front seat. Walter Franks is the young man on the running board. He was one of five boys raised by a mother after their father's death. The father was an early-day freighter in the Bend country and owned his own teams of horses and wagons. Courtesy of the *Bend Bulletin*

For twenty-five cents a barrel, Bend residents received fresh river water at their back doors daily. Barney Lewis, who had taken up the timber claim three miles west of town where a brickyard would be established later, and Lucky Baldwin had both been watermen so it is hard to tell which one is filling the water barrels in this picture, taken where Pioneer Park is now. Horses and cattle still went to the river to drink.

Barney Lewis, who came to the country in 1905, wasn't a cattleman like Allen, Staats, and Todd. He wasn't a ditchdigger either, or a lumberman. A good painter who dabbled in oils, he liked to paint pretty pictures of the mountains. Unlike the others, he built himself a house with lumber and painted it green. The small, two-room house was always referred to as the "green house," when all the other houses were built at the brickyard.

He painted signs for the stores in Bend, and the streetsigns. From the author's collection

This photograph was taken at the back door of the Hugh O'Kane Hotel before the fire in 1905. Ernest Smith, hotel clerk, is on the left side of the picture. Hugh O'Kane is wearing overalls and boots. Others in the picture are unknown. O'Kane was a lightweight prizefighter before coming to Bend. He is remembered sitting in an armchair in front of his hotel, a fat man who was always sleeping. He married later in Bend. Courtesy of Madge Smith Glassow collection

All this, $14.95

50 pounds Granulated Sugar
1 sack Flour
10 pounds Coffee
10 pounds Rice
20 bars "Diamond C" Soap
10 pounds smoked bacon
10 pound box Macaroni
10 pounds of Prunes
10 pound box of Crackers
5 pkgs. Borax Wash. Powder
4 lbs. loose Muscatel Raisins
15 yards Calico

All the above and more too at

The Bend Mercantile Co.'s ... Store ...

H. C. Ellis, manager of the new Deschutes Telephone Company, is shown with the company lineman, Ernest Smith, driving his 1902 Holsman. This photograph was taken in front of the telephone office, next door to the Bend Hardware. The date of the picture is unknown, but because the streets are paved, the photo must have been taken much later than 1905, when Bend received its first telephone service. Smith later purchased the Holsman from Ellis. Courtesy of Madge Smith Glassow collection

A news item in the *Bend Bulletin* in 1906 read that work on a new telephone line to Rosland had been completed and plans to construct a line to Sisters was in the making. Rosland, which changed its name to LaPine about 1915, was a growing town in the heart of the timber country, and many believed it would surpass the population of Bend. The hotel in Rosland was a popular stopping place for freighters going to the Summer Lake Country. When Bend started growing, many moved up from Rosland, including some stores. Courtesy of Cora Sather collection

Bend taxpayers voted three times to build a new school, each time increasing the size and cost of the building. As the enrollment increased from 47 to 103, the cost increased from \$3500 to \$6500. Although Central School had three stories, only the first floor, three classrooms, was used at first by the three teachers when the school was started in September 1906.

Finally, the high school was moved to the attic. After the first high school was built adjoining Central School, the student body continued to increase so some classes were moved back to the basement in this old school in 1916. Courtesy of the *Bend Bulletin*

This picture shows May Belle Reed and a friend in a fishing camp on the Deschutes River in 1906. The young ladies are wearing bloomers, named for Mrs. Amelia Bloomer, who believed that women should free themselves of the cumbersome long skirts and petticoats. Shorter bloomers worn under the dress were popular with younger girls who were beginning to take up sports enjoyed by their brothers. They might even show their black bloomers when hanging upside down from jungle bars or turning cartwheels. Courtesy of Madge Smith Glassow collection

Cowboys from nearby ranches and anyone else who thought he had a fast horse tried out in the Fourth of July horse races. This one, in 1908, had a good crowd watching from the sidelines on Wall Street.

None of these horses were thoroughbred racehorses. Most likely they had been running free on the range with the race turning into a bucking contest between horse and rider. Most of the horses in these races were the small, wiry cayuses only a few generations away from the Arabians brought over to Mexico from Spain, which had found their way into the Oregon country. Indians from Warm Springs often entered their fastest ponies in these races. There were no entrance fees and no prizes, but one could usually find someone to make a bet on his favorite horse and rider. Courtesy of the Oregon Historical Society

Who were the drummers in this July 4th band in 1908? Claude Kelley would like to know. The fife player was Ernest A. Smith. The picture was taken near the corner of Oregon on Wall Street, beside Lara's store. Courtesy of Claude Kelley collection

The Aune Livery Stable and Feed store was built in 1908. The Aunes specialized in heavy draft horses and furnished the logging teams for Shevlin-Hixon, which was still logging with horses. The stable was a big barn that took up half the space on the south end of Bond Street between Oregon and Minnesota.

Brooks-Scanlon finished cutting their timber south of Bend at the beginning of World War I. They built a logging railroad to their holdings in the Sisters and Metolius areas. Railroad logging ended in 1950 when both companies started hauling with trucks. At first they hauled over their own roads, but they now use public highways. Courtesy of Claude Kelley collection

At the time of this photo, Nick and Cora Smith had two sons, Lester and Elmer. Marjorie was born later. The family is watching a friend water his team above Staats's water wheel about where the Tumalo bridge would be built. Courtesy of Marjorie Smith collection

On March 20, 1908, a wireless message was received at Mare Island from a battleship 2,600 miles away. This was the first wireless received on the Pacific Coast from a warship. The fleet was on its way from the East Coast to San Francisco before beginning a long trip around the world by way of Cape Horn. This was President Theodore Roosevelt's goodwill tour around the world. From the author's collection

Oregon law in 1907 set a limit of 125 trout in one day from the Deschutes River. The penalty for surpassing the limit was not less than 50 dollars and not more than 100 dollars. Fish fries in Drake Park were often featured during Fourth of July celebrations.

These Dolly Varden trout came from the Deschutes River at Pringle Falls. The fisherman in this 1910 photograph are, from left to right, Henry Whitsitt, Jack Kelley, Tom Triplett, and LeRoy Fox. Courtesy of Claude Kelley collection

Eight horse freight wagons are pictured here coming into Bend. Note the bell tower on the white schoolhouse, so the picture was taken sometime between 1904, when the school was built, and 1906, when the bell and tower were removed for the new Central School. Undoubtedly, a load as heavy as this one went around by Prineville from the train at Shaniko to miss the steep grade at Trail Crossing, on the Crooked River. Courtesy of Claude Kelley collection

James and Violette Reed were pioneers in 1904. This photograph of them was taken in the 1920s. They bought property on the hill east of the present *Bend Bulletin* Building and the railroad tracks, on Division Street. It was here that they raised their family and where their granddaughter, Madge Smith Glassow, now lives in the still nice, well-kept home built by her grandparents. Courtesy of the Madge Smith Glassow collection

This is the Reed and Steidl sawmill in about 1908. Logging was done with horses and horses hauled the logs to the sawmill on low logging wagons. Courtesy of Madge Smith Glassow collection

The Reed and Steidl sawmill is shown here with the beginning of a sawdust pile. One slab has been cut off the log by the circular saw. The log will be turned before the sawyer, behind the log, runs it through the saw again. The log must be turned on the carriage in order to cut off a slab from the other side before beginning to cut lumber. Courtesy of Madge Smith Glassow collection

This third automobile to reach Bend was driven by H. H. Davis in 1908 or 1909. Davis was the brother of Mrs. Kelley who is in the back seat holding the baby. Her daughter, Susan, and son, Claude, are in the back seat beside her. Hugh Kelley is beside the driver. The car had two cylinders and a chain drive engine under the front seat. It was built too low to the ground so the driver often drove beside the road rather than get stuck on the high center. The tires were hard rubber with no inner tubes to absorb the bumps.

The car left Bend and two days later it was in The Dalles, 130 miles by modern highway. If they had gone around by Prineville instead of risking Trail Crossing the trip would have been twenty miles further. They took a steamer on the Columbus River from The Dalles to Portland and a train from there to the World's Fair in Seattle. Claude bought his first folding camera at the fair for twenty dollars. Courtesy of Claude Kelley collection

The Bend Commercial Club lined up to try out the new Bend-Burns road, expecting to meet the Burns Club halfway. The six men hired to grub out the 135-mile road across the desert with picks, shovels, and hoes had not had time to clear it of sagebrush and larger rocks in the time allotted between April 11 and 23, 1911. The two motor groups were to meet on the 23rd, but the Burns group failed to show up.

Of the shops shown here, only the N. P. Smith Building, the two-story building on the left, remains and is still in use.

The motorists are identified from right to left. First Jackson car: Prince Staats, driver; E. A. Sather in back seat with derby hat. Second Jackson car: Carl Hunter, driver; E. M. Lara is beside driver. Third car: occupants unknown. Hudson car: C. S. Hudson, driver (First National Bank President); Baird, passenger. Fifth car: "Pop" Hartford, driver; Taggart, passenger (owner, Taggart Hotel); Dement, passenger (Bend Hardware). Sixth car: George Palmer Putnam, driver. Seventh car: American Flyer, passengers and driver unknown. Courtesy of Cora Sather collection

These drivers are waiting to join the ten-automobile caravan that was to meet the Burns Commercial Club. From the author's collection

Lara's mercantile store was located on the northeast corner of Wall and Oregon streets. This 1909 photograph was taken soon after the store was built. Ruth Caldwell and one of the Kelley girls are on the sidewalk. A J.C. Penney store was on this corner for many years until 1982 when it moved to Boyd's Center Mall.

The old Lara's mercantile store was torn down to make room for the Penney store in 1932. Courtesy of Claude Kelley collection

In 1909 almost every girl in Bend rode on this Liberty Float to represent the forty-eight states in the Fourth of July parade. Ruth Caldwell stood beside the flag as the float was driven down Minnesota Street toward Wall Street. Courtesy of Claude Kelley collection

One of the first substantial buildings erected in Bend was built for Alexander Drake by N. P. Smith and a man named Oliver. It was constructed using handmade shakes and nails freighted in from Shaniko. The lumber was some of the first to be cut at Drake's sawmill. This is a later picture, taken about 1930, after Wall Street was paved.

This building, along with all of Drake's holdings, was sold in 1911 to Clyde M. McKay of the Bend Company. Remembered way out on Wall Street, possibly the first Miller Lumber Company location on the corner of Wall and Tumalo streets, which was "way out" at that time. Courtesy of Marjorie Smith collection

Nick Smith worked for a time as a carpenter before moving to this house near the corner of Hawthorne and Oregon streets, catercornered from the present Chamber of Commerce house. Cora Smith is shown here with baby Marjorie, Nick, and their sons, Elmer and Lester. This rock wall is similar to the Drake wall. Courtesy of Marjorie Smith collection

Flossie Reed Smith was the new bride of Ernest A. Smith in 1909. Courtesy of Madge Smith Glassow collection

Mrs. Hall's Hospital, built in 1909 across from the Baptist church on Oregon Street, had no more than three beds.

Fern Hall, Dr. U. C. Coe, and a nurse are shown in front of the hospital. This was Bend's first hospital and it was in use until Mrs. Hall moved to Portland in 1914. Dr. Coe moved to Bend from Prineville once he had the use of this facility for his patients. Courtesy of Madge Smith Glassow collection

Marjorie, daughter of N. P. and Cora Smith, was the first baby to be born in a hospital in Bend. Courtesy of Marjorie Smith collection

With no football games to watch on TV on Sunday, young people went walking and climbing. This is Paulina Peak south of Bend. From the author's collection

Inga and Cora Sather are shown here riding along the Deschutes wearing divided riding skirts. Noone could ride side saddle on an Indian cayuse. Courtesy of Cora Sather collection

This is the first Catholic congregation to meet in their own church—they bought the one-room schoolhouse that was located on Wall Street. In 1910 an addition was built on, but the little church became crowded when the big mills brought many new people. Nevertheless, it served the congregation for another ten years. The schoolhouse stood on the hill north of where the present Deschutes County Courthouse now stands. Courtesy of the *Bend Bulletin*

The second location of the *Bend Bulletin* was in the Lawrence Building at the end of Wall Street, between Franklin and Minnesota streets. The staff shared the building with the public library. A gate was made for Luddemann, the editor, to reach his house. It wasn't needed for long because he was soon married and moved to Antelope. He had a chain of Central Oregon newspapers. This photograph was taken while there was snow on the ground. Courtesy of Marjorie Smith collection

Waiting for the parade on the southeast corner of Wall and Oregon streets in 1909. Taggart's Confectionery was across Oregon Street from Lara's mercantile store.

Bend had a parade in winter, in summer, and anytime a dignitary arrived, which was not often. Note the wooden sidewalk and the boy with a *Saturday Evening Post* bag. The *Post* was delivered to customers, not mailed. There was not one woman in the crowd and not enough snow for a sled. Courtesy of Marjorie Smith collection

Mrs. Kelley (married women were always addressed that way, and not by their first names) and Mary, a visiting cousin, are shown standing in the front yard with enough fish to feed the large Kelley family. Mrs. Kelley is on the left. Courtesy of Claude Kelley collection

This is a sage grouse cock displaying before hens. Homesteaders and city folks found these sage grouse an appetizing addition to many meals and found a variety of ways to prepare them. Courtesy of Fish and Wildlife Service, Department of the Interior

The entire Bend High School, and the seventh and eighth grade classes, went on a picnic in 1910. Courtesy of Claude Kelley collection

Bend's first football team had its first out-of-town game in Prineville in November 1910. The thirteen players and coach furnished their own clothing including shoes, sweaters, and helmets. Those who could not afford a helmet played without. Most played without. They each chipped in fifty cents to buy their $6.50 football. Admissions and contributions paid for a hired hack. The principal threatened the team with expulsion for playing hooky, but he was talked out of it by parents and townspeople. The team spent two nights in Prineville, one before and one after the game. Courtesy of Claude Kelley collection

This is the home town baseball team about 1910. They played a Prineville or Redmond team and played by themselves for local entertainment. They were all young Bend men. Courtesy of the Claude Kelley collection

During a cold spell, a skating rink was created between Wall Street and the Troy Laundry in early February 1910. Courtesy of Claude Kelley collection

This photograph shows E. A. Sather and his children Ted and Gladys, in the back of the Sathers's home. The two oldest Sather daughters, Inga and Cora, still live in this big white home, the finest in Bend when it was built. The smaller building, probably painted red, no doubt was the Sathers's barn. Courtesy of Claude Kelley colleciton

This is the 1909 wedding photograph of Miss Lilian Wolfe, daughter of Mrs. Charles Niswonger of Bend, and Fred Van Matre, who came to Bend in 1903. He learned the stonemason trade from Charles Niswonger, who later became Bend's first mortician.

Van Matre, Fred Hunnell, and Arthur Gertsen bought the timber claim of Barney Lewis, an artist, and started making hand molded bricks. It was a slow and tedious job, so they were more than willing to sell their brickyard to the new arrival, A. H. (Arthur) Horn in 1910.

No more bricks were made there until a brick machine could be brought in on the first train in late 1911. Years later, after Van Matre had learned the bricklaying trade and had become a successful Bend contractor, he and Ham Miller of the Miller Lumber Company bought the old brickyard and made brick only for their own use.

Marjorie Van Matre Anderson (one of seven sisters) and her husband, Donald, now live on the place in the redesigned house where the author grew up and spent her first years of married life.

Don Anderson is the son of Mr. and Mrs. Emil Anderson. The Anderson brothers, Emil and Fred, and Emil's family came to the Bend country in 1905 and built a sawmill on the old Sisters road that passed the brickyard and crossed the Tumalo Creek at the Indians' crossing. Their sawmill was between the town of Sisters and Tumalo Creek. Courtesy of Clara Van Matre Anderson collection

One of President Theodore Roosevelt's last signatures before leaving office in March 1909 went on a bill that made three forest reserves that could not be traded for worthless railroad land elsewhere. One of these reserves was the timber southeast of Bend that Sidney (S.A.D.) Puter tried to steal. This reserve included 6,300-foot Pine Mountain. Courtesy of author's collection

In this 1911 photograph, a freight wagon has just brought in a supply of hardware from the railhead at Shaniko. The N. P. Smith family and deliveryman pose to have their picture taken before it is unloaded. This hardware store building is the only original building left on Wall Street and the only wooden business building left. It was built by N. P. Smith in 1909 and has always belonged to the family. The Smiths lived in the upstairs apartment that is still occupied by their daughter, Marjorie, who taught in the Bend schools until her retirement and continues to be active in many civic affairs.

The Deschutes Historical Society placed a historical marker (plaque) on the building in May 1977. Courtesy of Marjorie Smith collection

This is a photograph of the interior of the N. P. Smith hardware store around 1910. Note the row of wood stoves, one with a warming oven. Smith also carried a good supply of copper-bottomed wash boilers and gun shells. The long stovepipe let him take advantage of all the heat the small heater put out instead of letting it go up the chimney . Smith stands behind the counter. This interior is now used by the Bend Shoe Clinic with no structural change. Courtesy of Marjorie Smith collection

The Nick Smith children, Elmer, Marjorie, and Lester, stand in front of their father's hardware store to have their picture taken in about 1911. Someone's Ford runabout also got in the photograph. Note the spare tire and toolchest on the fender in case the car had a flat tire. There is room on the back for extra supplies instead of the rumbleseats enjoyed by the younger set. Courtesy of Marjorie Smith collection

This is the Bend-Shaniko stage on Shaniko Flats in 1910. Courtesy of Claude Kelley collection; photograph by John Linster

The Bend Water, Light, and Power Building was built on the corner of Wall and Franklin streets. This company was incorporated in 1904 and is owned by the city of Bend. The construction of the plant did not begin until 1909. Services did not start until one year later, when this photograph was taken. Water is still unmetered in Bend, but when there has been a light snowfall in the mountains so that water is scarce, a short-term law in the middle of summer forbids watering lawns and gardens except in early mornings and late evenings.

Some privately owned, 800-foot wells shared by close neighbors supplement the city water for irrigation. Thomas Foley, father of Robert Foley, county judge, was the first manager and served many years with this still city-owned public utility. Courtesy William Van Allen collection

This 1910 photograph shows a ten-horse team hauling the turbine and large wheel for Bend's first electric power plant. Notice the bells on the lead horses. These bells warn other wagons on the crooked Cow Canyon road. Arnold is on the rear horse with the jerk line. Ralph Dunn and Jack Kelley own the horses. The wagon is coming into Bend on Greenwood, nearing the dam that furnishes Bend's power. Ralph Dunn is standing by the big wheel. The other men are too small in this photograph to identify. Courtesy of Marjorie Smith collection

The Kelley Building on Wall Street, between Oregon and Minnesota, was in part of the space now occupied by the First Interstate Bank. The small door opened into Kelley's candy and cigar shop. It was the only place in town that sold fresh fruit. (No doubt the fruit was hauled in from the cove.) In the back was Claude Kelley's darkroom where he developed most of the pictures taken in the area from 1910 on for a number of years, including his own and all of Susan Horn's. In this photograph, the football team is coming out of Turpin's, a restaurant and ice cream parlor. This building burned down, and when it was rebuilt, Corkett's took over two rooms for an ice cream parlor. Courtesy of Claude Kelley collection

Wall Street is shown here after the sprinkling wagon has given the road a good soaking in order to settle the dust. Clarence Sather is watching from the sidewalk near the Sathers's store. C. S. Caldwell's store is the tall building next to Sathers's toward Oregon Street across from the low real estate office. Courtesy of Claude Kelley collection

Walter Combs built the Bend Garage on Wall Street, next to the north end of the Old Pilot Butte Inn in 1910. After his ride on a freight wagon to the gold fields in eastern Oregon, he decided automobiles would be needing a lot of repairs. He had sold a fine span of black horses and had gone along to the gold fields to keep an eye on them until he received his pay. This 1914 photograph shows the garage before it was re-established south of Franklin Street. The garage was moved when the new Pilot Butte Inn was built. Courtesy of Clyde McKay collection

Here is a 1910 view of Wall Street across the Newport Dam. Linster's new dance hall and skating rink (the white building) burned down soon after it was built and was never rebuilt. Possibly that is the Linster residence next to the dance hall. To the right of the dance hall is a view of the back of the Pilot Butte Inn after the first addition was built. Central School is the white building in the distance. Courtesy of Claude Kelley collection

This is the Newport Street dam just north of Newport Bridge. It furnishes Bend's electricity. The power house is in the upper center of the photograph. This dam holds back the water in the Deschutes River, forming Mirror Pond. Courtesy of the Claude Kelley collection

Wall Street can be seen beyond the new power house and dam. The new Newport Bridge is on the right. Note the boardwalk leading up to Wall Street from the bridge.

From left to right the buildings are the Pilot Butte Inn, with the addition that later became the Colonial Inn, the Drakes's home (nearer the river), and a home that became the Lumberman's Hospital (later Saint Charles Hospital). Courtesy of William Van Allen collection

The Bend Flour Mill, built in 1911, advertised high patent, straight grade, whole wheat, graham, or rye flour in 1913. It also advertised grits, breakfast food, bran, shorts, and all kinds of feed. Bend women complained that they couldn't make good bread or cake with the mill's flour, and that their grits were too gritty. However, diners on the Oregon Trunk Railroad were served Bend's rye flakes, and the Benson Hotel, Portland's best, also served them. Furthermore, in 1917 samples of rye flakes were sent to Herbert Hoover, America's food connoisseur, and the local farmers could not supply the demand for Bend Flour Mill products.

The flour mill company also sold agricultural implements, such as wagons and other farm machinery, but financial troubles caused the mill to be closed. Finally the building was used as a warehouse by the Deschutes Farmers' Association. On July 5, 1940, a fire of unknown origin started in the old warehouse and jumped to the Oregon Trail Furniture Plant, a brick structure that originally housed the Bend Steam Laundry, built in 1913. Photograph by Susan Horn

Members of the Bend Ladies Riding Club join an early-day parade in 1911. Courtesy of Art Camera Shop

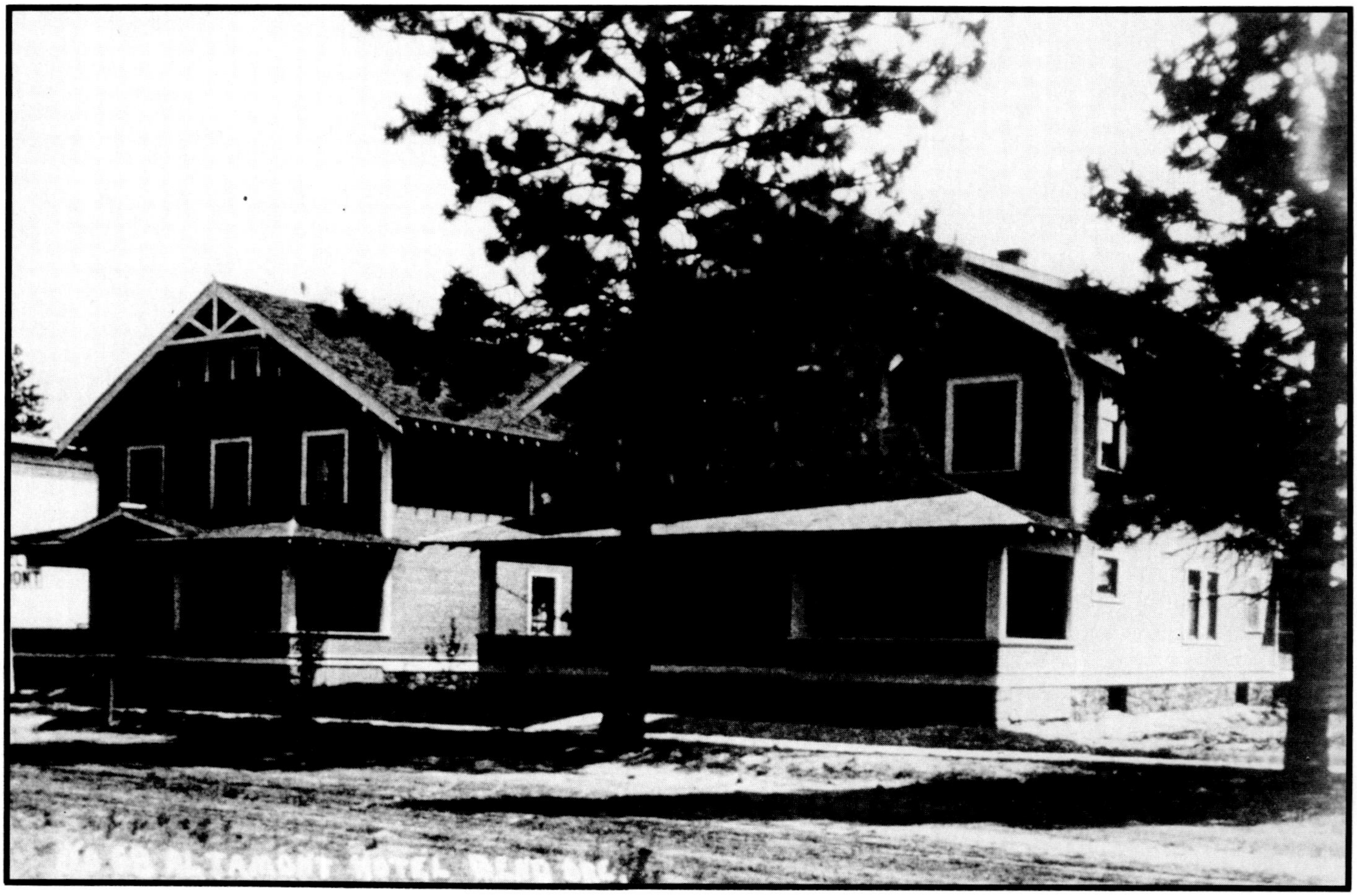

The first hot water system in Bend was put into the residence of Mr. and Mrs. A. T. Frame in 1911. It heated every room in the house. Next door is the Altamont Hotel or rooming house, managed by the Frames. It barely shows on the extreme left of the photograph. Courtesy of Clyde McKay collection

"The Church at the head of downtown Wall Street"

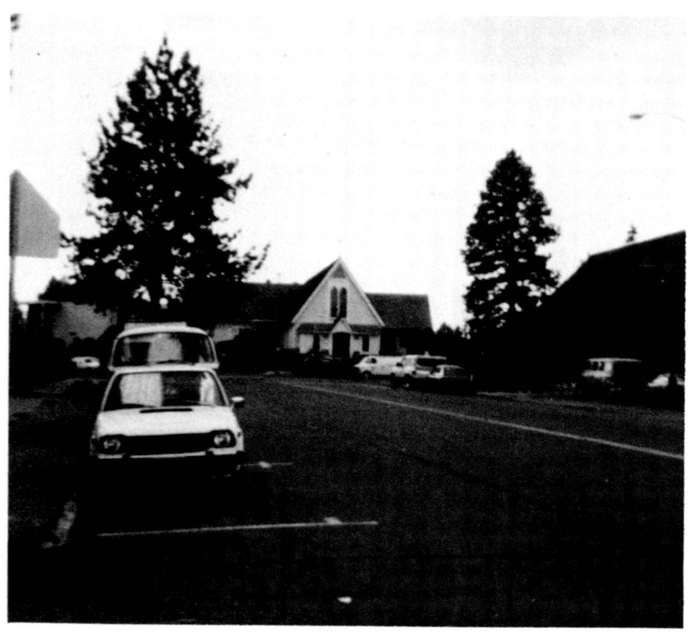

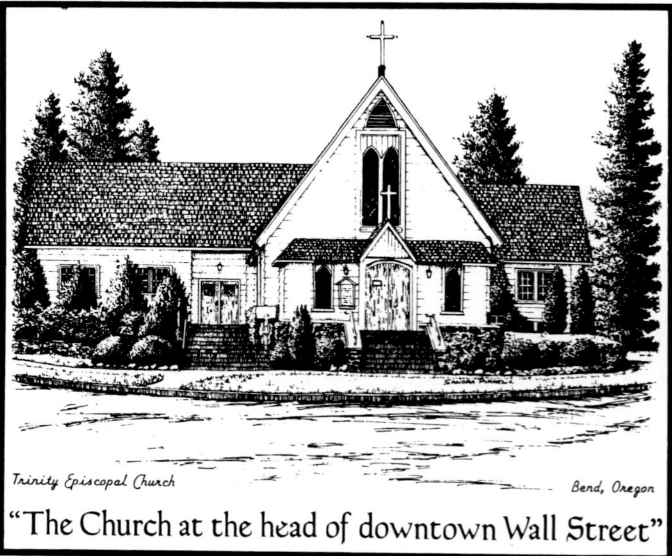

Clyde McKay, representing the Bend Company, bought all of Drake's property in 1911. Mrs. Drake withheld the lot at the end of Wall Street for an Episcopal church. For many years this lot was vacant, forcing traffic on Wall Street to go around it at an angle to continue south to Saint Helens Place. From the Trinity Episcopal Church Bulletin

Clyde McKay was the manager of the first mill owned by the Bend Company. He was also responsible for bringing the first big wheels for logging to the Bend country. Courtesy of Clyde McKay collection

Low-wheeled log wagons hauled logs to the Bend Company mill. Low wheels made loading logs onto a wagon easier. Courtesy of Clyde McKay collection

George Palmer Putnam tries riding western style. Putnam, son of the New York publisher, bought the *Bend Bulletin* in 1910, the year this photograph was taken. Putnam was the heartthrob of Bend girls until he went back to New York and returned with his bride.

He wrote many articles promoting the Bend country and was the author of *Salting the Rocks*. Putnam left the *Bulletin* to become Governor Oswald West's private secretary. Divorcing the wife who was known in Bend, he married the American aviatrix Amelia Earhart who was the first woman to fly around the world. On her second flight, this time alone, she disappeared and was never heard from again. Courtesy of Claude Kelley collection

Louis W. Hill, son of James J. Hill, who was president of the Great Northern Railroad Company. He was in Bend in May 1910, promoting central Oregon's land settlement. Here he holds a swath of alsike clover. Courtesy of Oregon Historical Society; photograph from the Spokane, Portland and Seattle railroad

In 1910 an exhibit of central Oregon products was assembled in Bend to be sent to a dry farming congress. The picture was taken by George Palmer Putnam who came to Bend to write a story about the railroads and stayed to buy the *Bend Bulletin.* The men in the picture, from left to right, are J. N. Hunter, John McClure, John Steidl, Sr., two gentlemen whose names are unknown, and Elmer Merrill. The Hunter and Staats Building, in the background, was on the corner of Wall and Newport streets. Courtesy of Claude Kelley collection

Before the trains arrived in Bend in late 1911, newcomers to the country either drove their own team and wagon, rode horseback, or took the train to Biggs, a lonely train station with a cafe attached set on a sand bank a few rods above the Columbia River. Here they waited for an engine, with a passenger car and a freight car attached, to back down out of a canyon to pick up passengers going to Shaniko, the end of the line. They stayed there overnight at one of two hotels, with toilets down the hall and breakfast family style.

The morning stage was a high, two-seated buckboard without a top. Before 1910 there was only one route to go to Bend. With dust rolling up behind and a wind bringing it back over the passengers, the stage headed for Cow Canyon, a ride the passengers found breathtaking. After a stop at Grizzly for a meal of brown beans and bread, the bus rolled into Prineville. This is a sixty-two mile ride by modern highway, but in the first decades of the twentieth century the road went around lava outcroppings instead of grading them down, so it was many miles farther. From Prineville there were still forty miles to go before reaching Bend.

The photograph shows Susan Horn on the right and the author waiting at Biggs for the train to Shaniko. As usual, in the Columbia River Canyon, the wind was blowing and there were many more men going to the new country than women. Susy was the only woman among the whole crowd of men. Bend was a good place for a single woman to go if she wanted a husband, but professional men were few. From the Author's collection

Bruce Igo, driving his 1912 model Ford around Bend, takes his sister, Beulah, for a ride. In the back seat, Irving Reed and Wanda Pigerou are enjoying the sunny afternoon. Note the small tires and the lamp. Courtesy of Madge Smith Glassow collection

V

1911-1915

George Palmer Putnam bought the *Bend Bulletin* and went back east to bring back his bride. The High Desert became dotted with homesteads with many small communities, each with its own post office.

The big news, as it had been the last of 1910, was the progress and fighting of the two railroads that were competing for the right-of-way up the Deschutes River Canyon and their arrival at Bend.

Women complained about the dust raised by the many sheep and cattle driven through town. A water wagon was put into use laying the dust.

Anticipating an influx of single men with the railroads and anticipated big mills, voters, all male, decided to let the thirteen saloons on Bond Street sell hard liquor instead of the near beer they were supposed to be selling during Prohibition. When the trains finally reached Bend on the same tracks, Bend had a big celebration.

"The Big Game Hunter," Teddy Roosevelt, returned from Africa hopping mad at the way his protege, President William Howard Taft, was showing his conservatism. Running against Taft on the Bull Moose ticket, Roosevelt split the Republican party and helped elect Woodrow Wilson president.

Germany was building up her armaments, perfecting the airplane and the dreadnought, refining her submarines and machine guns. The Kaiser's legions were strutting a built-up militarism through universal conscription. The Archduke of Austria was assassinated, a good excuse for a wholesale declaration of war, one country against another. Germany invaded France and Belgium. Britain said that the invasion of Belgium was a violation of an almost century-old treaty and declared war on Germany.

Bend people took sides, some insisting that it was none of our business. They blamed or praised Wilson for "keeping us out of war." Homesteaders were waging a war of their own against an invasion of jackrabbits that ate everything in their path. Instead of guns, the homesteaders used clubs. Townspeople joined them for the sport or to help friends.

The train brought in brick machinery, and in the spring of 1912 Bend started building with brick instead of lumber. Bend also got clusters of streetlights, stronger than any in Portland. Through the efforts of Abigail Scott Duniway, women voted in Oregon and in Bend in 1912, eight years before the Nineteenth Amendment was passed in the United States.

Almost everyone laughed when Wiest subdivided his homestead and called it Wiestoria, Bend's first subdivision. Hugh O'Kane was snoozing out in front of his hotel and Fourth of July parades were followed by horseracing down Wall Street. Most of these local cayuses wore Obe Riley's OR brand.

Mare Island Navy Base in California received a wireless message from almost 3,000 miles away before President Roosevelt's goodwill tour of naval craft started around the world. Roosevelt had also signed a bill before leaving office that put the timber Puter attempted to steal into a forest reserve, that could not be traded off for railroad scrip.

A road between Bend and Burns was supposed to be finished when Bend's Commercial Club planned on meeting a Burns group halfway.

Bend had a hospital where women could go to have their babies, and Dr. U. C. Coe moved from Prineville to be in attendance. Claude Kelley had a darkroom behind his father's candy and cigar store where he could develop pictures taken by other camera bugs like himself, pictures that he has generously shared with this author.

At the end of 1911 Bend had 384 school-age children, an increase of 86 percent over 1910, and the greatest increase in any city in the United States, according to the *Bend Bulletin*.

Here a homesteader leaves for the high desert, taking all of his belongings. Photographer unknown, from the Author's collection

Millican, twenty-six miles southwest of Bend, was the first stop to many high desert claims between 1910 and 1920. George Millican sold water to thirsty travelers for five cents a cupful and twenty-five cents for a tubful of water for their livestock. Homesteaders from many miles around filled their water barrels at Millican's deep well for only a nickel a barrel, hauling two barrels at a time. Water was pumped up by a handmade windmill. George Millican also had bunks to rent for the night in two small shacks. He furnished straw-filled ticking, but the traveler furnished his own bedding.

The Post Office Department finally discovered in 1953 that Millican was a one-man town and took away his post office that was used by travelers wanting his postmark. Courtesy of Claude Kelley collection

An ingenious use of rocks for fence posts was also a way to clear the land on the desert. One strand of wire, that failed to keep the jackrabbits from going under and the antelope from going over, was all that was required by the government to prove up. Long before that time, most of the homesteaders had moved to Bend to find work or to establish businesses. Some of them had left the country altogether, leaving nothing to show they had ever been there except an occasional fence post or a flat, lava rock cornerstone of a shack. Neighbors who had not yet starved out had been over to pick through the debris for anything that might be useful almost before the wagon disappeared over the first hill. But some stayed. Millican, and Bill Brown, who lived closer to Burns and back in the hills. Bill would have a big spread, become rich and die poor. And Half-way will be there under different ownerships as long as people drive cars and need a place to eat and rest and a cold drink of water from a deep well. From the author's collection

Irrigating by hand was hard work. Water doesn't run uphill. Ditches had to be dug a little deeper and the water pulled along with a hoe until it began to run freely. Then water was started down the next row. Courtesy of Clyde McKay collection

The spectacular Fort Rock formation is in semi-arid High Desert country near Bend. Loose material of an ancient volcano was removed by the waves of a Pleistocene lake, leaving the strange rim, several hundred feet high and nearly a mile across. Early homesteaders chose the Fort Rock area first. Water was close to the surface, and the soil rich, but they soon discovered that a thin sheet of alkali came to the surface when they tried irrigating. Homesteads were soon abandoned.

It was in the Fort Rock area, in Cow Cave, where moccasins made from sagebrush were found, dating back several thousands of years. Since then, other artifacts have been found under a deep layer of cinders showing that man once lived here, chipped his arrowheads, and ate his meat, leaving animal bones but none of his own, and leaving one wondering if they escaped that great holocaust to become ancestors of the present-day Indians, or did they succumb to some other disaster? Fort ROck became the immigrants Chimney Rock in the prize winning movie *The Way West.* Fro the author's collection

This buyer was not too enthusiastic about the typical ranch fence. From the author's collection

People who could afford to buy segregated land with water rights from a canal usually could afford a better house than those who lived in shacks. This house was even close enough to timber for the owners to gather their own firewood and material for fence posts. From the book with author's collection

If a farmer was lucky, he could get a good crop of hay, provided that the jackrabbits didn't get to the young green shoots first. Baling required several farmhands and a baling machine, and, usually, some onlookers. The baler and his man went from ranch to ranch as hay became ready. Only the large ranchers could afford all the equipment needed to harvest a crop. Quite possibly the baler belonged to Bill McNaught in the Alfalfa area around 1911 or 1912. Courtesy of Mae McNaught Gladish collection

A rabbit drive is taking place in the snow in this photograph. There were too many jackrabbits to shoot, and besides, ammunition cost money. Friends and neighbors lined up with clubs and drove the animals into a low ravine or just circled them and clubbed them to death. Those they missed multiplied. The experience of one drive was enough for the fainthearted, until the rabbits descended on the first green garden shoots. The rabbits were even good eating until they were discovered to have liver worms. Courtesy of Clyde McKay collection

Here is a ten-horse freight outfit, driven with a jerk line (note the rider on the rear horse). The outfit is hauling a steam boiler for an irrigation project at La Pine. The photograph was taken on the corner of Bond and Greenwood, the site of Frenchie Estebenet's Waldorf, Bend's first recreational center, for men only. Courtesy of Claude Kelley collection

In 1910 a *Bend Bulletin* news item read, "Mr. and Mrs. Ben McCaffery, who recently took over the Bend hospital, are being kept busy these days. There are now four patients in the hospital." Dr. J. C. Vandevert bought this hospital. It served as his home overlooking the river. It has now been torn down, and the property is used for a free parking lot. Courtesy of Clyde McKay collection

The Hill and Harriman competing railroads were staying on their own side of the Deschutes River Canyon until they reached Sherrer's Bridge. Here, on Sherrer's homestead, the canyon was too narrow for two sets of tracks. After several deals and lawsuits that delayed tracklaying for almost a year, hired thugs and dynamite experts were brought in and the war started. It was especially bad when rattlesnakes were dynamited down on the crews.

Finally, the railroad heads had to agree, and they finished the climb up the canyon with one set of tracks. The Deschutes was sixty feet deep at Sherrer's Bridge.

This was the old Indian crossing where

Ogden lost his horses and broke down the Indian bridge. Courtesy of Claude Kelley collection

Anticipating an influx of single men when the railroads arrived, Bend's 153 male voters, in almost a tie vote, voted the town wet. That meant that the twelve saloons that were serving near beer could begin serving hard liquor. When one saloon burned down on Bond Street, endangering the town, and at the same time the Log Cabin Saloon opened its doors, the city fathers decided twelve saloons in a town the size of Bend were enough and that no hard liquor could be sold away from Bond Street except with meals. This made Hugh O'Kane roaring mad because this meant that only the Pilot Butte Inn could serve liquor. His Bend Hotel had no dining room. After that, some said that his near beer was as potent as the real thing.

The photograph shows Albert Taylor in his bearskin coat, with his son, Sylvester, in front of the new Log Cabin Saloon on the corner of Bond and Oregon streets. From the author's collection

When there was a shooting on Bond Street (the fella just wanted to see the man dance) and a man fell out of an upstairs window at Mrs. Mac's Millinery Shoppe, the new Governor, Oswald West, threatened to send in the National Guard to clean up the town After that, the *Bend Bulletin* editor, George Putnam, carefully toned down the sensational news or omitted it entirely. This is a 1914 photograph of Governor West. Courtesy of Cora Sather collection

A tent city sprang up overnight on the north edge of the Crooked River Canyon. It was called Opal City after the opal springs a couple of miles downriver. Many people from Bend went to see the train come in at Madras and to see the progress on the bridge.

The Horns went to pick up Robert Colver, who had bought into the Bend Brick and Lumber Company. He bought some land in the Alfalfa area with money from selling his dairy farm in Seattle. The Walter Scotts also bought a share in the company. Standing at the uncompleted approach to the canyon are, from left to right, Bill McNaught, Susan Horn, the author, Mabel Scott, Nona McNaught, and Mae McNaught. Standing behind Susan Horn, almost out of sight, is Bob Colver. Art Horn took the picture. From the author's collection

Working both ends of the railroad bridge over Crooked River Canyon, workmen went up and down the almost perpen-dicular canyon walls on rope ladders. The canyon was 320 feet deep. A fall could mean instant death, for there was nothing a man could catch hold of. Material and equipment used on the south end of the bridge were transported up the river a couple of miles to Trail Crossing. This road had been blasted out of the side of the canyon only a few years before the railroads reached Crooked River. There were few turnouts blasted out along the side of the road where vehicles going down could turn out and wait for the vehicles going up. Once stopped on their way up it was almost impossible to get started again. The front team always wore a string of bells to warn oncoming drivers. Once down at the bottom of the canyon and across the narrow bridge over the river, even knowing horses pricked up their ears to listen for the bells before starting up the steep and twisting grade.

Never before in the world had a bridge spanned a distance of 340 feet without a trestle. The actual bridge work was started on June 26, 1911 and was not completed until September 25, 1911. From the author's collection; photos by Art's Camera Shop

This crowd waited at Redmond, twenty miles north of Bend, to see the train come in there a few days ahead of the Bend arrival. Notice the small house on the right for emergencies. Redmond was a new town and grew quickly after someone discovered that the rich soil would grow big potatoes. When the Frank Redmonds took up a homestead there in 1904, they were the first in the area. Two years later, they were holding their first Deschutes fair. Courtesy of Clyde McKay collection

In less than a month, the depot and the right-of-way into Bend were donated or paid for by public-spirited citizens. Fifty-two leading businessmen contributed cash in amounts varying from five dollars to $525. The land was donated. The pink stone used to build the depot came from a deposit southwest of Bend. The depot is no longer needed, so it is now used as a feed store and for storage. Courtesy of Marjorie Hoover Tromblee collection

The train whistle coming from a distance had an eerie sound. This first train was unusually long, for it brought many officials and important people who wanted to make that first run. Later trains rarely pulled more than a single passenger car, except for the night run that had a pullman with several freight cars hooked on behind. From the author's collection

Over 2,000 people gathered for the ceremonies in Bend on Railroad Day, October 5, 1911. There were water sports, bucking contests, horse racing (down Wall Street), foot races, a baby show, a parade, a smoker, and dancing during the two-day celebration. Bend had long anticipated this important day, although regular passenger and freight service did not start until November 1. The *Bulletin* bought a Linotype machine and Weist had waited for the train before sending for his grandfather's clock, built for his grandfather in 1804. Courtesy of Clyde McKay collection

Wall Street was smoothed down and beautified to welcome visitors coming in on the train later in the day. Note that there are two land offices ready to do business. Wall Street was the main street of the town but was never officially called Main Street. Courtesy of Art's Camera Shop

James J. Hill, age 73, led the Railroad Day Parade. As president of the Great Northern Railroad Company, he drove the golden spike of the Oregon Trunk Line earlier, marking the end of railroad track construction at Bend. Courtesy of Oregon Historical Society

Here is part of the sophomore class of Bend High School as they waited in front of Central School to join the parade. Harry Spinning is driving, and Helena Bozell is standing. Seated on the school desks are Claude Kelley, Ella Sandord, and Clyde McGillvery. Courtesy of Claude Kelley collection

That first train brought the Bend Brick and Lumber Company's brick machinery. From the author's collection

That first train that brought in the brick machinery took out the first load of lumber to be shipped from Bend. It was the first of a million-dollar order to go to the Midwest. Owners and members of the mill crew that loaded the lumber were, from right to left, Art "Red" Brinson, who married Edna Boyd; Neiley; Arthur "A. H." Horn (in the white shirt); and Walter Scott and Bob Colver, owners of the brickyard and sawmill. Henry ("Hen") Goodman (next, with his hands in his pockets) was a brother-in-law of the Scotts, and had just come in on the train. The two men on the end are unknown. The sawmill was moved over to the brickyard soon after the brick machine was set up and a deep well was drilled.

Later, the Scotts wanted to go back to Vermont, and Bob Colver preferred dairying to brickmaking and sawmilling. Colver took the Scott ranch and his own ranch. Scott was bought out, and the Horns again owned the company. From the author's collection

When Walter Boyd and Hen Goodman arrived from Vermont, they wowed the local girls with their ready-made Fatima cigarets and the small plush rugs that came in the packages. Every girl in town vied for these rugs and wanted a sofa pillow made from them. From the author's collection

Waiting to greet a Seattle delegation coming in on the new train, these Commercial Club members were ready to stage an old-fashioned train holdup. The participants were, from left to right, George Jones, George Palmer Putnam, Harper Skuse, H. E. Allen, John Steidl, Ward Coble, Vernon Forbes, J. P. Keys, Clyde McKay, and Tom Foley. They relieved the visitors of their wallets and valuables but returned them later at their meeting, to the relief of many present. Courtesy of Clyde McKay collection

Members of Bend's baseball team have cooling refreshments at the Palms after a game. In the photograph, Howard Young is on the left. Behind Young is Hunter (first name unknown). Ivan Thorsan has the soda, and Lyle Richardson is coming in the door. The young women are unknown. The picture was taken in 1911. Courtesy of Claude Kelley collection

Filling a brick kiln took a good eye and a good pitching arm. Fred Kottwick is catching the dried bricks that Joe Grey is pitching. Photograph by Susan Horn

Arthur Horn insisted on taking one shift of twelve hours himself when burning brick, to be sure the fire never got too hot. Fire that was too hot would burn an arch down so the heat couldn't get through. Large logs unfit for lumber were split to burn in the kiln. Families at the brickyard and friends from town often spent their evenings around the kiln, watching the fire, roasting marshmallows and hot dogs, and telling stories and singing songs.

A second kiln on the extreme right is being filled for a later burning. Arthur Horn is on the right with the spade; the helper on the left is unknown. From the author's collection

Fire in the wooden buildings was always a worry in early Bend. Heating was by wood stoves, even in banks. Hotels, including the Pilot Butte Inn, had small heaters in every room. The firemen were volunteers who left their places of business and rushed to their stations.

In 1911 the thirty-three volunteer firemen elected E. A. Sather, a leading groceryman, to be their fire chief. They also elected other officers. they decided the best place to keep their chemical cart was at Eagleston's hardware shop on Wall Street, as near the center of town as possible. Hose cart number one would be left on Minnesota Street. This might have been on the street where it would be handy. Hose cart number two would be somewhere on either Bond or Wall Street. A big fire could always bring a crew from the nearby sawmills. Their whistles, tied down to blow continuously, would drown out the ringing of the fire bell, but they would alert the whole countryside. Courtesy of Clyde McKay collection

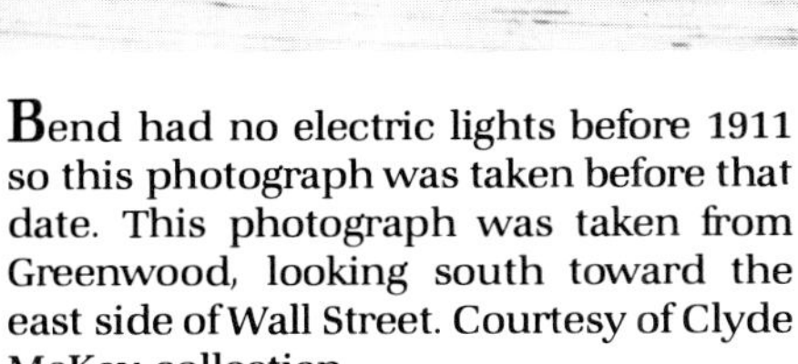

Bend had no electric lights before 1911 so this photograph was taken before that date. This photograph was taken from Greenwood, looking south toward the east side of Wall Street. Courtesy of Clyde McKay collection

The circus came to town the summer after the train first came to Bend. The parade came up Wall Street and turned onto Greenwood. The small building in the photograph that can be seen between the wagon and the horses is probably Boyd's butchershop. It is located catercornered from the Pilot Butte Inn. Lara's is the tall building across Oregon Street from Taggart's Hotel and candy shop. Circuses and chautauquas were always set up on the east side of Wall Street on the empty lot south of Lawrence Street. Even though one rode a horse to work or to school, it was always fun to ride the merry-go-round and "whoop it up." The men were drawn to the "girlie-girlie" shows, but when they left, they looked sheepish for having been so gullible. Courtesy of Marjorie Smith collection

This photograph of the east side of Wall Street was taken looking north from Oregon Street. At this time, either Lara's or the store next door was selling gasoline by the five-gallon can—the pump was a later innovation. The street was filled with rocks that were dragged down by the two teams. Courtesy of Clyde McKay collection

This photograph shows the northwest end of Oregon Street with Lara's store facing Wall Street. W. C. McCuiston put Lara's old awning to use. The Skuse building was one of the first brick buildings to be built after the brickyard began making bricks with the new brick machine in the summer of 1912, yet before Bend had electric lights. These buildings face Oregon Street. Courtesy of Clyde McKay collection

This is a photograph of the east end of the north side of Oregon Street after electric lights were installed. The Log Cabin Saloon was between the bank and the Baptist church. J. A. Eastes branched out into the real estate and insurance businesses. Courtesy of Clyde McKay collection

This is the south side of Oregon Street in 1912 after lights were installed. Fire destroyed this Kelley building along with Hugh O'Kane's hotel in 1915. The A. L. French Building, menswear, was one of the first brick buildings constructed in Bend. Taggart's Hotel was on the corner. The Deschutes State Bank, with Mr. Baird as president, replaced the wooden building on the southwest corner of Wall Street. The man with the hose is just settling the dust. Courtesy of Clyde McKay collection

This photograph shows a block of ice being hauled up from the Arnold Ice Cave about 1912. The cave is a part of the old Deschutes River bed cut off from the original stream during some early eruption. Rain and snow water pouring into the cave makes a perpetual supply of ice that is no longer taken out because of modern refrigeration. From the author's collection; photograph by Susan Horn

This fine two-story brick building occupied by the Deschutes State Bank replaced a wooden building on the southwest corner of Wall and Oregon streets in 1912. It was the beginning of a brand new look in the center of town. The free public library found quarters in a back room of the bank building, its door opening on Oregon Street. It would be the library's third move. New cluster electric lights were installed on the bank's corner in 1911 along with other clusters about the main streets of town. The Mode O'Day shop now occupies the corner of this brick building. Courtesy of Madge Smith Glassow collection

The fair at Redmond has always been an exciting time. Vegetables and grain are measured, judges taste cakes and pies. In the first few decades of the twentieth century wild horses were gathered in a corral ready for the big event of the day. Local cowhands rode broncos right off the desert, so they never knew whether the horse would buck or run, make long pitching jumps, or stand in one place and whirl. Everyone rooted for his favorite rider and groaned when the animal just stood and did nothing. Time was measured by the number of seconds a rider was able to stay on.

The Indians from Warm Springs always had a good audience watching them play their stick game and trying to outguess the players who were passing a small stick around their circle of participants. The players bet on who would have the stick when the game ends.

Redmond was an upstart of a town twenty miles north of Bend, with the nearest house at Cline Falls, three miles away, when Frank Redmond settled there in 1904. Two years later, the town of Redmond staged the first Deschutes Fair.

This picture is from a 1963 edition of the *Big Haul*, now out of print. The fair has been an annual affair continuously since 1906. Courtesy of the *Big Haul*, 1963

These boys were the honor guard in the 1912 Fourth of July parade. They are standing on the corner of Wall and Minnesota streets. The boy on the left is Elmer Smith, and the third boy is Lester Smith. (They were sons of Nick and Cora Smith.) The other two boys' names are unknown. Courtesy of Marjorie Smith collection

This 1915 photograph shows the location of the brick plant and the sawmill east of the brickyard (right, above) belonging to the Bend Brick and Lumber Company. The author's childhood home was off the photograph further to the left and below. From the author's collection

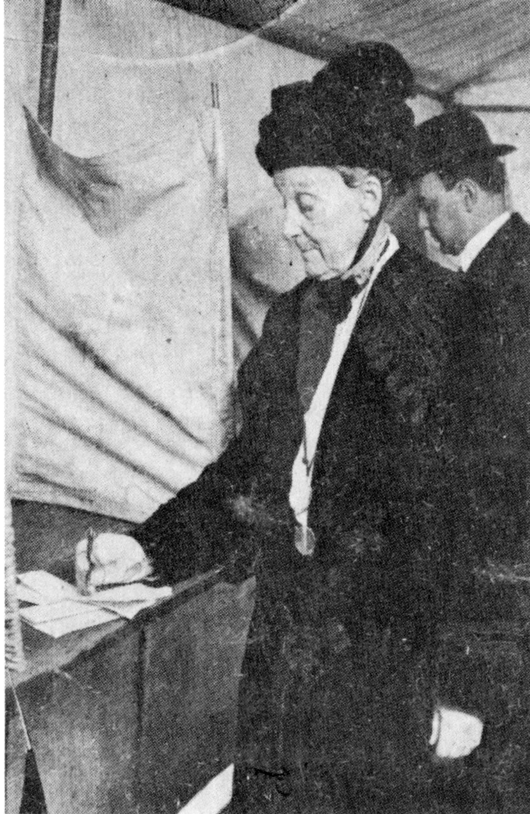

In 1912, Abigail Scott Duniway was the first woman to vote in Oregon. After a long, hard fight, she persuaded Wyoming and Idaho to grant women suffrage before her own state adopted it. Courtesy of *The Oregonian*, April 30, 1976

Eighty thousand sheep were shipped out of Bend in 1913. Most of them were herded down Wall Street from the Tumalo Bridge to Greenwood and on to the freight depot. Women rushed to close their windows when they saw the sheep coming because the animals raised a terrible dust, worse than the frequent whirlwinds that raced through town. Courtesy of Clyde McKay collection

Cattle, too, stirred up the dust on Bend streets on the way to market. Courtesy of Violet Mayne Franks collection

This East Third Street in 1936. People laughed when "Old Man" Weist cut up his homestead into city lots and called the area "Weisteria." The big Weist home was built about two blocks north of Greenwood. Mrs. Mayne's nursing home was new when this photograph was taken. The Cook residence can be seen in the distance. An unidentified building is being built between the nursing home and Weist's residence.

The Dalles-California Highway goes through Bend on this street. The small houses that were on the east side of the street have all been replaced by business buildings, fast-food restaurants, and motels. The Weist house was demolished to make room for a service station. Mrs. Mayne's hospital has been made over into several small apartments. Kate Rockwell, the famous Klondike Kate of Alaska's gold rush days, lived on the east side of the street after she moved into Bend from her High Desert homestead. Courtesy of Violet Mayne Franks collection; photograph by Myron Symons

This is a candid camera shot of Mrs. Franks going to the barn to look after her horses. Widowed, with five boys to raise, she took a homestead in the High Desert in 1913 where she lived until 1916, when she proved up. Most of these homesteads turned out to be worthless and went back to the government for the taxes. Some of this land close to the hills was rented out for grazing land to stockmen. The buildings disappeared during the years or were torn down by neighbors for the lumber. All five of Mrs. Franks's sons, John, Walter, Louis, Oscar, and George, made their homes in or near Bend. Courtesy of Violet Mayne Franks

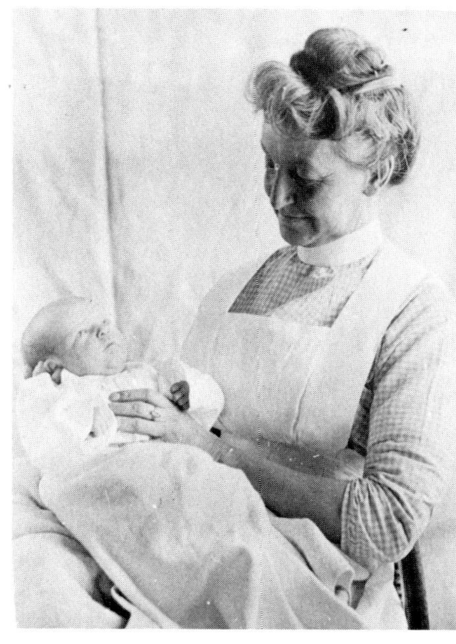

Mrs. Fern Hall is holding Beulah Onst, who came all the way from Prineville to be born in Mrs. Hall's hospital in 1914. Courtesy of Madge Smith Glassow collection

In 1915 the Fourth of July parade progressed north on Bond Street. Later that summer the Bend Hotel burned down completely during the night. The next year Hugh O'Kane constructed his building on that location. Courtesy of Claude Kelley collection

This stately Central Oregon Bank on the corner of Wall and Oregon streets was sold to the Lumberman's National Bank sometime after Hugh O'Kane constructed his new building on the other end of Oregon Street in 1915. Lumberman's changed the looks of the building by closing off the corner door and adding doors on both streets. Lumberman's merged with the United States National Bank, losing its identity. Courtesy of Marjorie Smith collection

Claude Kelley ran the projector for this second movie house in Bend. It was built on Bond Street by L. C. Rudow in 1915 and was called the Dream Theatre. The first movie house ran occasionally over top of Sather's mercantile store on Wall Street. Courtesy of Claude Kelley collection

Marjorie Hoover Tromblee waits at the wheel beside the Bend Water, Light and Power Company to enter the 1915 Fourth of July parade. She is driving a new Ford that is all decorated for the occasion. Courtesy of Marjorie Hoover Tromblee collection

This is a photograph of the Torrence (Tom) Foley family taken in their Haines automobile about 1915. Mr. Foley is in the driver's seat with Robert (Judge) Foley beside him. Mary Ellen is in the back seat with her mother, who is hidden by shadow.

The Foleys came to Bend in 1910, across the Santiam Pass from Eugene, Oregon, in a covered wagon. They took up a desert claim near Hampton Buttes but moved into Bend when Tom oversaw the building of the dam and powerhouse. He then became manager of the Bend Water, Light and Power Company, a position he held for many years. Courtesy of Judge Robert Foley collection

There was no turning around on McKenzie Pass until you got to Windy Point, even when you had to get out and do a bit of roadbuilding with rocks and brush where the road had been washed out. From the author's collection

Bend - 1916 - Copy - Photo Art

The 1915 Fourth of July parade went south on Wall Street past McCutchen's Hardware across Oregon Street and the bank building on the corner. Patterson's Drug Company and R. M. Smith Clothing Company are visible in the distance. Some of the businessmen had put in cement sidewalks. Bend claimed three miles of sidewalks at this time, but some were just single boards. Courtesy of Claude Kelley collection

Here we look from Harmon Park across the Deschutes River above Newport dam and Newport bridge. Seen under a branch of a willow tree is the Pilot Butte Inn.

VI

1915-1920

The Shevlin-Hixon Company announced in 1915 that it would be building a sawmill west of the Deschutes River and that it would be employing 500 men as soon as its mill was completed in 1916. The Brooks-Scanlon Company announced a week later that it was beginning to build, that it would hire 500 men the next year, and that it would be hiring more as soon as its box factory was ready. The Shevlin-Hixon mill would be the largest operation in the lumbering business in the world. The two companies built across the river from each other, with Brooks-Scanlon building just south of Farewell Bend Ranch.

Workmen flocked into Bend by the thousands looking for jobs. Tents went up beside the canals, along the Deschutes, on Staats's property, just north of where Brooks-Scanlon was building its mill. Hammers pounded far into the night, building houses for the newcomers. The two mill companies built a dam between them for log ponds. The official 1916 census count showed that Bend had the fastest increase in population of any place in the nation. Bend people were disappointed when Jefferson County was cut out of Crook County, but in December 1916 Bend had its own Deschutes County, with Bend the county seat.

Europe was at war. German submarines sank several American ships. Many Americans were angry. Some wanted to get in it, but "He kept us out of the war," and Woodrow Wilson was reelected. He hoped he could get the two sides to settle their differences. British and French cavalry officers were in Central Oregon buying horses.

" 'Peace, peace,' the Kaiser says," newsboys shouted on the streets, hawking the *Bend Bulletin*'s latest special edition.

Three small one-room buildings were built on the school grounds east of Central School. They housed the fourth, fifth, and sixth grades. Miss Holmes taught all three grades, moving up with her class as it progressed from room to room. It left her behind when Reid School was built.

Henry Ford was paying workers five dollars a day. Art Horn said that if Ford could do it, so could he. The going wage at the big mills was three dollars and a quarter a day for an eight-hour shift. Any boy or girl in Bend or at the yard who wanted to earn a little money could turn bricks or stack pallets for fifty cents a day. It wasn't until after they had grown up that they realized bricks didn't neet to be turned to keep them from cracking in the sun on days they wanted to go fishing or go on a picnic.

The banks in Bend stayed open until ten o'clock on Saturday nights so the mill workers could cash their paychecks. No one ever locked their doors. There was no need to. No one ever went swimming in the Deschutes River or the Tumalo. They were too cold, coming right out of the mountains. Children either walked to school or rode horseback and took their horses to the river to water at noon or rode in Myrl Hoover's school bus. They rode horseback to Sunday school also and tied their horses to the hitching rack outside. There were a few cars around, but they were not just for driving by the young people in the family. Out to Pilot Butte was just a nice walk after church. It was hard on the shoes if they decided to climb to the top. It was no easy job pulling oneself up by holding onto a sagebrush and slipping back one step or more for every one going ahead. It was always a race to see who could get to the top first. It was no problem going down through the loose cinders. Going out to the Tumalo from town was less strenuous than climbing the Butte, but it was a four-mile jaunt each way. Then there were the apple trees, long since rotted away. That was down the river a mile or so past the Pioneer park.There never were any apples on the trees that Dr. U. C. Coe and Mary Collins planted sometime after the turn of the century.

Bend had a week of chautauqua the summers of 1915 and 1916. They set up a big tent on the corner of Wall and Franklin streets and the children learned songs and a play that they would present the last afternoon. The children squirmed while speakers talked above their heads during the evening while they waited for the travelog. A mother would get up and leave at the most interesting moment, for even fretting babies were not left at home with babysitters, even if one could be found who would miss chautauqua. It was a week to remember. Then came the war.

War was declared April 1, 1917. Every boy in the Bend High School thought the "call to arms" meant him. Some of these boys were older, making up for lost time spent on the High Desert, where many teachers had not gone beyond the eighth grade. Almost every boy in the 1917 football team rushed to enlist, and not all were old enough, even when they fibbed a little about their ages.

Uncle Sam soon found he had too many young boys, and few older heads. He also found he was not ready, even though the young men were. He lacked clothing and shelters. A draft brought the men in as needed. Young men signed up when they came of age at twenty-one. Older men up to age thirty-six registered immediately. Many husky loggers were disgruntled when they were put in a Spruce Division and sent to Newport, on the coast of Oregon, to cut down spruce trees. Lightweight spruce lumber was needed for the framework of the new airplanes that were being used to fight the war.

Many boys were sent overseas half trained and thrown against the enemy, the Germans. They were all boys, no matter what their ages. Percy Stevens went down on the *Tuscania* before he reached Europe, Bend's first hero.

Everyone sang England's "Tipperary" until Irving Berlin wrote "Over There." New songs came out fast after that. Sweethearts sang "It's a Long, Long Trail" when words failed them.

Women rolled bandages from old bedsheets and made man-sized hospital gowns and knitted socks, sweaters, and wristlets. Schoolgirls took their knitting to class and dropped stitches. Some women went to work in Brooks-Scanlon's box factory, taking what had previously been a man's job. Some went to the fruit orchards to pick fruit that would otherwise go to waste. They Hooverized and saved their three pounds of sugar to make candy or cookies for someone in service. They waited at the post office for the mail to be sorted. They watched the bulletin boards outside the *Bend Bulletin* and *Oregon Press* offices, watching for the latest news and reading the casualty lists. Some went home to change the blue star on their service flag hanging in the window to one of gold. They wrote letters to boys they didn't know.

They sold and bought Liberty Bonds, gave "til it hurt," and gave some more. They refused to have German measles—they had "red" measles. There was one German in town who talked broken English. Some patriotic zealots wanted to ride him out of town on a rail. He gave more than many from his meager salary. Wiser heads put a stop to such talk.

Many caught the Spanish flu and died. The flu was no respecter of age or health. It took those in the prime of life as quickly as the old and sickly. Women put on mouth and nose masks and went to the gym to take care of the overflow of influenza patients from the hospital.

Then it was over, the flu and the war. Bend celebrated a false armistice, just like the rest of the country, and had to do it all over again.

The men in the employ of the Brooks-Scanlon Company voted just before opening time in the afternoon to quit for the afternoon, and the men in the Shevlin-Hixon plant did not wait for that formality.

At noon the whistles of the two plants screeched their welcome to the news, and automobiles with cutouts open and horns honking raced through the city streets. The women employees of the Brooks-Scanlon Lumber Company paraded the streets with a coffin containing an effigy of the Kaiser; crowds thronged the streets and gathered around the bulletin boards.

It was a great day in Bend.

Early in the evening crowds began to gather on Oregon Street, and at eight o'clock several hundred people were gathered around the Liberty Temple, where speaking was to take place.

R. P. Minter, enthused over the end of the war, announced the day the greatest in the history of the world. When he referred to the "greatest American of all time, Woodrow Wilson," he was interrputed with cheers.

R. C. Hamilton was introduced and spoke a few minutes on the more serious side of the problem which the city was facing at that hour, that of putting her quota over the top in the United War Work drive which was languishing in the city.

He declared that war or no war it was a duty that every citizen owed himself and to his nation to get his name in the Honor Roll for this fund.

In the midst of his remarks, he was interrupted by a messenger asking him to announce to the crowd that there was a fire in the Windmill poolroom and that the firemen were desired to report for duty. The entire assemblage evidently considered themselves members of the fire company, for in about two minutes Hamilton was talking to the wind, and Bend's impromptu celebration was ended.

And then it all had to be done over again.

A cartoonist drew a picture of the world with its head bandaged up and holding up the right hand, saying "Never again," and people believed that and went on about their living.

Some returning veterans met new sons and daughters born while they were away, some married sweethearts who had waited for them, and some brought home French and English brides. There was a baby boom in 1920. Many veterans were ill, suffering from the poison gas they had breathed in the trenches while in France, but there were no veterans hospitals to take care of them and no money to pay for their care.

Alex Mayne built a new house on Kansas Street and Hattie Mayne opened the Mayne Hospital to care for all the mothers who would be having babies. The Pine Tree Tavern opened for business at the west end of Oregon Street, on the riverbank. It would not be serving liquor.

Many ex-service men were out of work. Times were hard and apples didn't sell very well on the streets. Many in Cox's army were hungry, tired, and ragged when they reached the nation's capital and camped on the White House lawn. Many of them were shot. They never forgot.

There was another group of men, mostly loggers from the West, who talked about better pay, shorter hours, and safer working conditions. They wore big lapel buttons with big IWWs on them. They said the letters stood for Willing Workers of the World. Some said that "IWW" stood for "I won't work."

A group of Bend veterans left an exciting rodeo at the ballpark to meet at eleven o'clock on November 11, 1919, the first anniversary of the armistice that ended the war, to organize the fourth American Legion post in the state of Oregon. They named the post Percy Stevens, honoring Bend's first war casualty. Their purpose was to care for their disabled comrades and their families. There were no veterans hospitals, only a meager allowance to reeducate for new jobs the most disabled. The government was slow in granting small pensions. Not until 1932 were the veterans' organizations able to persuade Congress to build a veterans hospital in Portland to take care of the disabled and other veterans unable to pay for their own hospital care.

The Ku Klux Klan raised its ugly head in this postwar period while patriotism was still high. A cross burning on Pilot Butte by hooded strangers who preached hate ended with them leaving town hurriedly.

The first meeting of the county officers was in the O'Kane Building. After his disastrous fire of 1915, Hugh O'Kane built this fine new building on the corner of Bond and Oregon streets. It housed a theatre that wasn't too popular with the ladies, because they hadn't quite overcome the idea that ladies didn't walk on Bond Street past all those saloons. The County Court continued to meet in the O'Kane Building, renting two rooms, until October 1917, when they moved into a new building on Bond Street across Oregon Street. From the author's collection

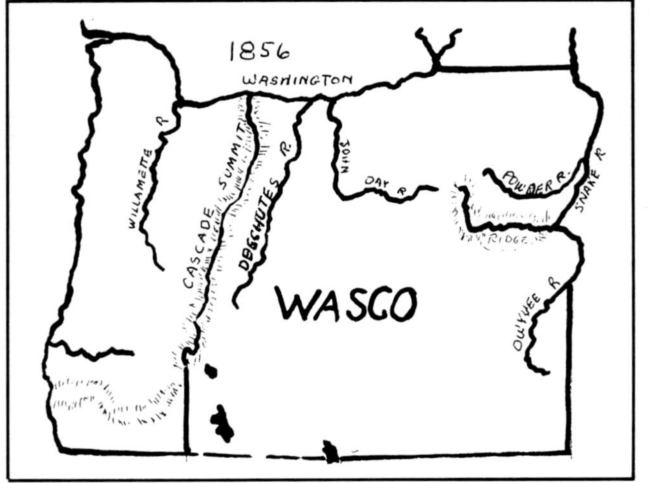

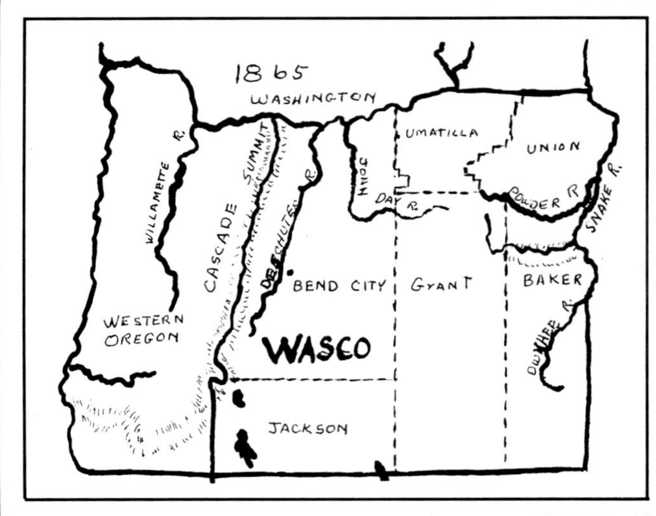

When Oregon was divided into counties, all the land east of the Cascades was called Wasco County. Gradually, as the rise in population demanded it, new counties were cut out of Wasco until only Crook County, in the center of the state, was created, with more land than there is in all of Massachusetts. Although Prineville, the county seat, was much closer to the growing city of Bend than was the town of Wasco, it was still a long day's drive by team or car, for those who had such transportation.

Bendites were disappointed when Jefferson County was carved out of the northern part of Crook County. Then in December 1916, Bend became the county seat of Deschutes County, the last county created in the state. Courtesy of Elsie Williams Roe

In 1916 Bend had two sawmills hiring five hundred men apiece. Shevlin-Hixon promised to build two more mills, making it the largest sawmill ever built. The milsl were built across the Deschutes from each other, above the Tumalo Street bridge. Brooks-Scanlon bought the old Farewell Bend ranch property and tore down the O'Neil school and old Sisemore or Todd log cabin for their second edition.

They divided their log ponds in the river with a cement divider. Brooks-Scanlon's on the right, Shevlin-Hixon on the left of the photo, with the first section or mill working. Sawdust and slabs were burned in the tall burners causing great plumes of smoke filling the air. From the author's collection.

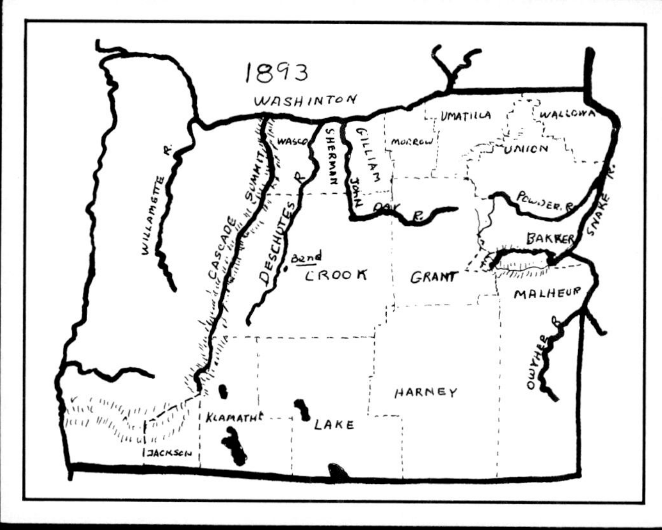

1893
WASHINTON
UMATILLA
WALLOWA
WASCO
MORROW
UNION
SHERMAN
GILLIAM
JOHN DAY R.
POWDER R.
SNAKE R.
WILLAMETTE R.
CASCADE SUMMIT
DESCHUTES R.
BAKER
Bend
CROOK
GRANT
MALHEUR
OWYHEE R.
HARNEY
KLAMATH
LAKE
JACKSON

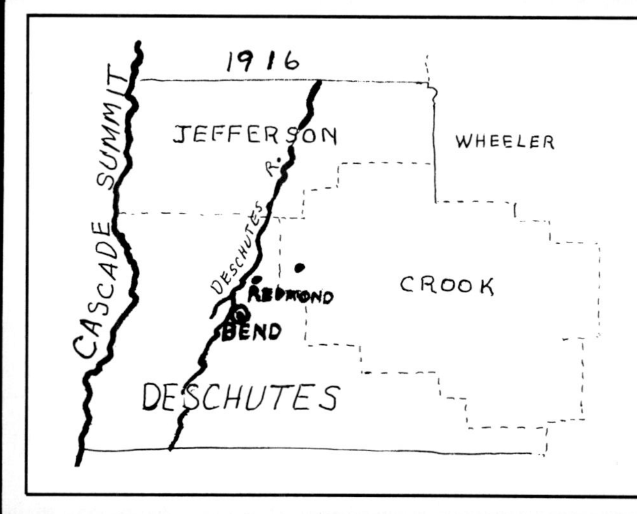

1916
CASCADE SUMMIT
JEFFERSON
WHEELER
DESCHUTES R.
REDMOND
BEND
CROOK
DESCHUTES

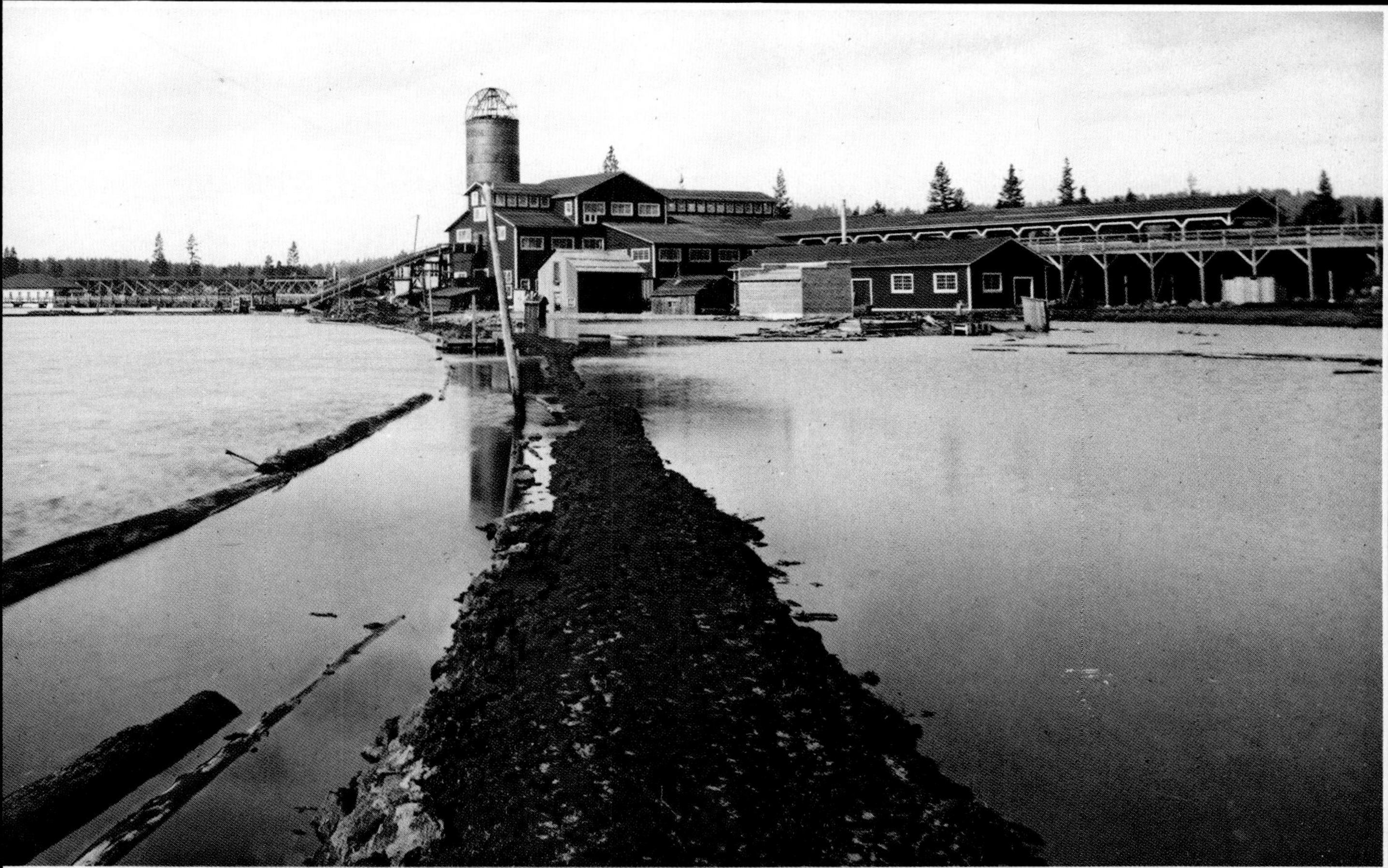

The Shevlin-Hixon's million-dollar burner was over 100 feet high, was built with fire brick four feet thick, and was covered with one-half and three-fourth inch steel plates. When the mill closed, the burner was scientifically dynamited, and the steel was sold to sheep ranches to be used for water tanks.

The private road and railroad trestle lead to the Shevlin-Hixon mill. Courtesy of Ray Van Vleet

Shevlin-Hixon is shown with the mills cutting. Streams of water wash logs going up the chutes, because dirt and debris dull the saws. From the author's collection

This picture shows Shevlin-Hixon's shop area with a good view of the Cascades. From left to right are South, Middle, and North Sisters; Mount Jefferson; and Mount Washington behind timber covered foothills. Photos by William Van Allen, from the author's collection

An unnamed Bend Bulletin reporter has his picture taken with an unusually large log ready to be pulled up a chute at Shevlin-Hixon's. From the author's collection

Two big logs start up the chute at Shevlin-Hixon's. From the author's collection

Clyde McKay, Superintendent of Shevlin-Hixon, overlooks the logging track and train in the Deschutes River Canyon north of Bend. Note the smoke-stack above the rock rim. From the author's collection

This is a Shevlin-Hixon logging camp used for families when timber to be logged is at a distance from town. When the timber is cut the camp moves on flatcars to a new location. A school and a company store is also moved. Courtesy of the Clyde McKay collection

Pete Hansen and U. H. Gless cut down a big pine with a crosscut saw, the hard way in 1918. Courtesy of Claude Kelley collection

These men are cutting a big yellow pine with a power saw. Photograph by Paul Hosmer

These unnamed timber fallers are cutting down an unusually large tree with a gas-powered saw. The man with the cigarette would be in trouble if he lit it. Courtesy of Pine Echoes

This big tree was too big to handle so Brooks-Scanlon intended leaving it for a tourist attraction. It died over the winter and it contained too much good lumber to waste. When the saw came to the center of the log and was too short to reach through, Guy Davis chopped out deep notches around the log to allow the five foot blade to cut through. Roscoe Sims, foreman, used his time to sharpen his axe with a file. They sawed all around the log first, leaving the center to cut last through the deep notches. Courtesy of Brooks-Scanlon's *Pine Echoes*

George Balitch, skilled powderman measures off places to bore holes for blasting powder while Roscoe Simcox, Assistance logging Superintendent bores the holes. From the author's collection

With only one charge going off the log was split neatly in half with very little lumber wasted and two halves much easier to load on flat cars.

Realizing that two mills could not keep cutting at the rate they were cutting, Shevlin-Hixons sold to Brooks-Scanlon. Later Scanlon sold his interest to Brooks. Brooks sold to Diamond Lumber Company. Shevlin-Hixon's shipping shed, all that is left of the big mill is on National Register of Historic Sites. Story and pictures from May 1946 issue of Brooks-Scanlon Pine Echoes. Courtesy of Rose Hunnell Steidl collection

Piles of lumber air drying at Bend Lumber Company sawmill. The big mills use dry sheds. From the author's collection

Big wheels are no longer used to hawl logs to a loading dock. They gaugh the soil and destroy small trees in their wake. From the author's collection

Loggers had a good sense of humor. This was known as the road to Hellangone. It was at the junction of the Davis Lake Road and a Brooks-Scanlon logging road. The sign points to several mountain lakes on the Century Drive outside of Bend. The Century Drive, a one hundred mile drive, passes seven beautiful lakes, with branch roads to several more lakes. It also passes the foot of Bachelor Mountain.

In the sixties Hellangone was supposed to be a settlement a couple miles from Waldo Lake, about as far out in the wilderness as one can get. There is now a road to Waldo Lake, a good fishing spot. From Brooks-Scanlon's *Pine Echoes*, July 1958. Courtesy of Rose Hunnel Steidl

Paul Hosmer, editor of the defunct Brooks-Scanlon *Pine Editor*, sat to have his picture taken at the butt end of a Western Yellow Pine log. The subscription rate, according to the caption near the front page of the small monthly magazine: "By mail—if you are a lumberman, ask for it. Local—you'll just have to borrow it from somebody else." It was worth borrowing. Now there are only a few left.

Paul was not only a fine writer, he was a good photographer and an outdoorsman. He had the ducks eating out of his hands. He knew every duck on Mirror Pond and knew when a strange osprey showed up, for he kept a pair of high-powered binoculars handy so he could watch from a big window in his Riverside Boulevard home.

Paul came to Bend as a young man following a stint in Colonel Greeley's timber regiment in the First World War. His nimble fingers played the banjo for many a dance in the Bend country.

Picture and excerpts from Volume 1, Number 1, *Paul Hosmer Echoes*, written and edited by friends of Paul's, including the famous teller of tall lumbering tales, Stewart H. Holbrook. Courtesy of Rose Hunnell Steidl collection

The Arthur Horn home, built in 1916, was the first house built on West First Street, north of Newport Bridge. It was one of the first bungalows. From the author's collection

These Civil War veterans no longer walked in the parades, but they enjoyed riding in the "new horseless carriages" and participating in Fourth of July and Memorial Day programs. In the front row are veterans Tweet, Finley, and Smith. In the back row are Perrine, Morgan, and Morrison. Absent for the photograph was John O'Neil. After his first wife died, he married an old sweetheart in 1920 in the A. H. Horn residence. Courtesy of Marjorie Smith collection; from the Deschutes *Pioneers' Gazette*

The photograph shows Madge Smith Glassow's uncle and his Ford touring car about 1916, with the top up and the handy tool box on the running board. Homer Smith is the little boy in the back seat. Courtesy of Madge Smith Glassow collection

One tragedy marred the building of the Reid School when George Brosterhouse, brother of Ed Brosterhouse, the contractor, fell from the top floor and was instantly killed. He had come to Bend with his brother in 1903, and together they built many residences and other buildings. This building served hundreds of students for sixty-five years before becoming the headquarters for the Deschutes County Historical Society and the museum. Courtesy of Deschutes County Historical Society

Reid School was almost overflowing before the first year ended. To make room for students, the next year the seventh graders were sent back to Central School. Courtesy of Marjorie Hoover Trumblee collection

George F. Hoover's 1916 consignment of Fords, is shown in front of their building on Greenwood, just east of Harrison Street. This was Bend's first Ford agency. With two sons and three daughters, the Hoovers lived above the agency when they first moved into Bend from their homestead on the high desert.

One can see just the tip of one of the three small classrooms that were the overflow from Central school. They held the fourth, fifth, and sixth grades. Miss Holmes, a pretty young teacher (the niece of Mrs. Sellers), taught each grade as they moved up. These classrooms were abandoned when Reid School was built. Courtesy of the Marjorie Hoover Tromblee collection

This photo of the old Hoover Building with a face lift was taken in 1982. Photo by the author

This shows Bond Street during the teens, looking south from Greenwood. The Land Ofifce was in the Wright Hotel Building, which opened off Greenwood. The tall building was the Winandy Livery Stable. It was torn down to make way for the Trailways station. Across the street was Downing's restaurant, the first building in Bend made with brick. Crooked tracks to the left of the empty wagon go over the hill past the future site of the County Court House. Bond was a saloon street, so possibly several of the small buildings were saloons. Ladies didn't walk down Bond Street at that time, except to cross Oregon to go to the Baptist church. The tall building two blocks down Bond was Aune's livery stable. The photo was taken about 1915. Courtesy of the *Bend Bulletin*

Hotel Wright and the hotel bar were on the corner of Bond and Greenwood. The first manager didn't last long, even in a wide-open town. Built in 1917, of local pink stone, it now houses several small businesses including a Trailways restaurant. Who left his buckboard on the end of Bond Street? Courtesy of Clyde McKay collection

The Cozy Hotel was built in 1919 on Greenwood between Wall and Bond streets. It was a nice, genteel place where ladies could go alone and could stay. At that time women alone were not welcome in many places or did not feel comfortable eating alone. Often, they needed a nice place to stay while looking for a boarding house. The Cozy served that need and often had permanent woman guests. From the author's collection

The Methodists' Little Brown Church, out in the trees, was dedicated in 1912. Up until then, combined Protestant Sunday school classes had been held in the Baptist church. The Methodists had rented a room in the Baptist church every other Sunday for their own church services.

By 1916 the Little Brown Church on the corner of Franklin and Sisemore streets was bulging with new members. The young people in the Epworth League built an addition, the boys doing the carpentering, the girls providing the "eats." From the *Historical Sketch of the Methodist Church of Bend, Oregon*, 1956

After outgrowing the first church, the Methodists built this one. Courtesy of Claude Kelley collection

No one remembers when this white house was built on a lava pile at the north end of Bond Street. Nor does anyone remember who owned the cleaning establishment. It is known, however, that the building was standing in 1914 (when this photograph was taken). There was a permanent jog in Bond Street. Courtesy of Claude Kelley collection

This almost new Pilot Butte Inn was moved a short distance in 1916 to make room for a new Pilot Butte Inn. As the Colonial Inn, this building took the overflow guests from the Pilot Butte Inn. Courtesy of Clyde McKay collection

The new Pilot Butte Inn is built in the style of a French chalet. It is famous because it has housed many famous people, including Eleanor Roosevelt when she was on one of her war bond selling drives. Irving Cobb wrote many articles about the Inn. Many leading magazines and newspapers lauded its beauty and service as equal to any found in the United States and in Europe. Later, movie stars made their homes here while making their pictures. This photograph was taken from the corner of Wall Street and Newport, possibly in 1917, when it was brand new. Courtesy of the *Bend Bulletin*

Huffschmidt and Dugan's iron works gave Bend more than the simple blacksmithing that had been furnished at Elmer Lehrman's blacksmith shop across from the Baptist church. The works had a pattern shop and an expert pattern maker to make new parts and weld old parts together again. The shop is still doing business under different owners. It is still Bend's leading iron works. Courtesy of Clyde McKay collection

These male high school graduates of 1914 were uncomfortable in stiff celluloid collars. The girls, not so obviously, were encased in tight whalebone corsets. The girls were (from left to right) Hazel Ordella Thorson (McGillvray) and Ruth Florence Caldwell (Coyner). The boys were (from the top left) Lloyd Kelley, Arthur C. Vandevert, LeRoy Schooler Fox, Robert Kearney Innes, and Hugh MacKaye Thompson.

Two of these young men's names appear on the Bend High School service flag: Lloyd Kelley and Robert Innes. LeRoy Fox was inadvertently left out. Hazel married Ivan McGillvray, a pioneer of 1905, and Ruth married Craig Coyner, a 1914 pioneer; both men were veterans. Courtesy of the Deschutes *Pioneers' Gazette*

The McKenzie Pass over the Cascade Mountains between Bend and Eugene was not always an easy three-hour drive. And the streams were not always bridged, as these 1917 photographs show. Usually even the high-centered Fords needed to be pushed through a number of creeks found on the way, but first the women were carried across to lighten the load. This is Arthur Horn carrying his wife Susan while Albert Taylor carries his wife, Mamie. The author was carried across the creek first so she could take the picture with her mother's Brownie camera. There was no place to turn around until they reached Windy Point at the summit. Then it was the same creeks to ford again on the way back. Before reaching this point everyone got out of the car to build up the road with rocks and tree branches where it had been washed out during the winter. From the author's collection

Coyotes waited for calves and lambs to be born, so the state paid a bounty on ears. These pelts would bring the best price if taken in winter at their prime. Courtesy of Joyce Tifft Gribskov

World War I was declared on April 6, 1917. This call to arms meant that almost every boy in this 1917 football team and other boys in Bend High School old enough, or good enough prevaricators to get in, would go to war. Some first names are missing from this old *Bend Bulletin* picture of November 3, 1917. The members in the top row, from left to right are Ralph Curtis; Howard Young; Marion Coyner; Coach Eric Bolt (who also taught Latin and Math); Edward Brosterhouse; and Norcott. In the middle row are Craig Coyner and Paul Brookings. In front are Grubb, manager; Sanders; Calvin Smith, and Van Coyner. From the author's collection

John Joseph Pershing was the American general of the armies during World War I.

SERVICE FLAG
B.H.S.

1. Craig Coyner
2. Percy Stevens
3. John Brick
4. Howard Young
5. Lloyd Kelley
6. Robert Innes
7. John Steidl
8. Steve Steidl
9. Eric Bolt
10. Claude Sanders
11. Robert Fulton
12. Ray DeyArmond
13. Lyle Richardson
14. John Bates
15. Emil Henkle
16. Max Richardson
17. Robert Horner
18. Thomas Fagg
19. Clarence Boyd
20. Clyde Rongey

These names were on the service flag hung in the study room in the new Bend High School with names of boys who quit school or were earlier graduates from school. LeRoy Fox and a few other graduates were unintentionally left out. From the author's collection

These new soldiers, in their ill-fitting uniforms and carrying wooden guns, lead Bend's 1917 Fourth of July parade. They were sent home on furlough to await camp facilities and proper equipment, for Uncle Sam was unprepared for war.

The Golden Rule Store, at the end of Minnesota Street on Wall, gave way to Wetle's, a women's dress shop, in 1923. The Windmill pool hall moved to Bond Street, and a florist shop took its place after Wetle's expanded to the small building next door. The pink stone building (on the left) was built in 1912 by E. M. Thompson for a furniture and music store. Courtesy of Claude Kelley collection

The Bend Water, Light, and Power Company float was in the 1917 parade exhibiting the new way and the old way—these residents who didn't have an electric stove were doing things the old way. Courtesy of Claude Kelley collection

There were no high-priced designers to build these floats for the parade. Mannheimer's float was employee produced. Courtesy of Claude Kelley collection

The students are waiting in front of Bend's first high school for the Bend Hauling Company to unload their pickup in time to join the parade. Notice the soldier boys overseeing the job. Courtesy of Claude Kelley collection; photograph by George Palmer Putnam

During the war, women and girls rolled bandages, went to the Red Cross rooms, and made hospital garments. Girls, while in school, knitted wristbands, socks, and sweaters for our boys overseas. Women donned overalls and went to work in the box factory and in sawmills. Mrs. Gracy was the only woman working in the sawmill at the brickyard. The author was a pugger on the brick machine, tempering the clay. From the author's collection

Here is the Baptist Sunday school float. Among the spectators on the sidewalk are Mrs. Foley, Mrs. Clapp, the young people's Sunday school teacher, and Carl Green, a member of the class. Across from the Baptist church is Elmer Lehman's blacksmith shop. From the author's collection

The gym was built in time for some of the liberty loan drives. When the athletic club became pressed for funds during the depression, it was turned over to the YMCA, then to school district 4 with a new free swimming pool added. This old gym is now the administration building for School District 1. The downstairs rooms are rented to a private, nonsectarian school. Courtesy of Clyde McKay collection

Almost everyone Hooverized and ate brown bread. They had meatless Tuesdays, one meatless meal a day and two porkless days. They had a fat-saving day and a sugar-saving day. The Allies needed the food because they were fighting the war and had no time to raise food. Sugar was to be limited to three pounds for each person per month. United States Food Administration home card, 1918; from the author's collection

On this troop ship, the U.S.S. Minnesota, Guy Wilson is somewhere in the second row. From the author's collection

BEND CELEBRATES CLOSE OF THE WAR ON U.P. DISPATCH

Whistles Blew, Men and Women Quit Work, Parades Are Held and Celebration Staged.

ALL MUST BE DONE OVER AGAIN

Fake Dispatch Relative to Signing of an Armistice Throws City Into Paroxysm of Joy.

Bend celebrates the end of the war. Courtesy of the *Bend Bulletin*

This well-camouflaged Northern Pacific navy ship was the first boat to go through the Panama Canal. The war was over by the time it was commissioned, but that July, 1919, it was going from the West Coast to pick up a group of high-ranking officers still in France. Built in a shipyard on the West Coast, it was small and fast with nice accommodations for its distinguished passengers. It stopped in New York to pick up volunteers for this special duty that gave them three days in Brest, France, while the officers' gear was being loaded. It was back in New York on August 13, 1919. Ira Williams, a Bend boy, was chosen for duty on this fastest round trip at that time between the United States and Europe. From the author's collection

This tense-faced suffragette is picketing the White House before President Wilson signed the Nineteenth Amendment. Suffragettes picketed, marched, staged hunger strikes, and got themselves jailed before they were given the right to vote. Courtesy of the Library of Congress

VII

1920-1933

Disappointed because Congress refused to sign his League of Nations treaty that six allies had signed, President Woodrow Wilson went on a speaking tour to tell the people about his fourteen points for lasting peace. Worn out, he had a stroke on the tour and never completely recovered. His wife, Edith Galt, whom he had married while in office after the death of his first wife, guided his hand while he signed necessary official documents. Many said that she had been acting president those last months when he refused to relinquish the office to his vice-president.

In 1920, Wilson signed the Nineteenth Amendment, granting women in the United States the right to vote, a right women in Oregon had had since 1912. Earlier, during the war, he had refused to meet with a delegation of women during a Women's Rights Convention in Washington, D.C. He had also signed the Eighteenth Amendment, proposed by Senator Volstead to conserve grain needed by the allies during the war. But the war was over and the Volstead Amendment was still in force.

A few people thought it was smart to carry silver flasks and to add hard liquor to soft drinks under the table. Several stills ("blind pigs") in the surrounding hills and out on the desert served less discriminating clientele. Made in copper wash boilers and run through copper tubing, it was rumored that this liquor would either kill or cure whatever ailed you.

What was later known as the "roaring twenties" really never reached Bend. Bend's young people were divided into two groups. Those who could attend public dances went to the Hippodrome, if they could afford the admittance. If they had a car and the gas they might attend one of the dances at an out-of-town grange hall, to the music of Paul Hosmer and his band.

Hard times were felt back east before they were felt on the West Coast. There was no need for anyone to starve in the Bend country who could cut a willow fishing pole and bait a simple hook with a worm, for the Deschutes was teeming with trout. The people ate venison, in season or not. They traded dressed jackrabbits to Portland for valley vegetables and fruit. The people on Skid Road in Portland didn't know or didn't care that the rabbits had liver worms. Those who knew said they were good protein when cooked. Country canners traded mutton for Willamette valley string beans. They wore hand-me-down clothes and traded toddlers' clothes for baby clothes and got by.

Franklin Delano Roosevelt promised a New Deal and was elected president in November 1932, but it was March 6, 1933, before the new president could take office. In the meantime, more people were thrown out of work, more people lost their farms, their homes, and their businesses because they couldn't make the payments or pay the taxes. Veterans, out of work, ragged, hungry, and crippled, marched on Washington, D.C. and camped on the White House lawn, asking immediate payment of their bonus certificates instead of waiting until they were due in 1945. President Hoover said it would wreck the country to pay them then and refused to see a delegation. Instead, he ordered the commander of the army to fire on the veterans and chase them out of town.

The stock market crash on New York's Wall Street was felt around the world. Rich men were suddenly poor. Men who had bought stocks on a margin were broke. Despondent men splashed on the New York streets after jumping out of fifth and sixth story windows. Banks closed their doors on long lines of people demanding to withdraw their money before many bank closings.

After the first few months of demobilization at the end of World War I, many ex-servicemen were walking the streets looking for work. Many were too ill to work after being gassed in the trenches or not completely recovered from wounds or other illnesses. There were no government hospitals where they could go. The war department took a second look at this problem and began releasing men slowly and then only if they had a letter from a former or prospective employer stating they had a job waiting for them. Out of this brickyard crew of twenty-two men at least eleven were ex-servicemen when this photograph was taken in the summer of 1919.

On the top row, left to right are: Ira Williams, the author's husband, a veteran; Jack Kribs, now a contractor in Bend; behind him, an unknown man; Joe Grey; Arthur Horn, owner of the brickyard; Guy Wilson, ex-navy; and Mr. Kribs, father of the Kribs boys (one without a hat peeking around from the second row, and the boy in front with the dog). All but the boy and the two older men standing in the second row were veterans. In the front row is an army man. Fred Kottwick is holding the brick mold. (He was an experienced brickmaker and too old for service). The next four men were veterans. Next to the end is Alvin Christianson also a veteran. The author's station when she worked during the war was up the ladder where the clay was mixed with water to the right consistency to form bricks. From the author's collection

Glen Gosney was another Bend soldier who also spent almost a year after the war was over guarding the Siberian border. He is the soldier on the left in this 1919 photograph taken in below-zero weather. These men in Siberia saw no fighting and wondered why they were there. It was considered a hardship post. From the author's collection

When the "boys came marching home," many were not marching. Some came home ill or crippled or both, with nowhere to turn. They came home one at a time to a waiting wife and a growing family, a son or daughter they had never seen, or a sweetheart who was waited.

The boys who had left and came back men knew they would have to take care of their own. The government had made no provisions for emergencies or long-time help.

So they started their own American Legion Post and named it for their friend and schoolmate, the first to lose his life in World War I. It was the fourth post in the state, Percy Stevens Post 4. The members pledged themselves to look after the families of theif allen comrades, and those who had not died but needed help. Later, they would march at their conventions and local celebrations, keeping step with the needs of veterans to show their strength to a government that had forgotten. They named Frank Prince, uncle of Percy Stevens, their commander. From the author's collection

Headline in the Bend Bulletin

Percy Stevens, Bend Boy, Tuscania Victim, Passes From Rollicking Boyhood to Sphere of Influence Through HIs Early Martyrdom.

Percy Stevens has not died.

He can never die.

His sunny smile is firmly fixed in our memories, his joyous laughter rings in our ears, and his spirit, released on its mission of duty, call with that of one hundred seventy more of his comrades.

This is not death.

It is life.

Miss Emma (Dot) McBride became the bride of Leslie Wright soon after his return from overseas at the end of World War I. She and her mother came to Bend first in 1919 with her uncle, who was a horse trader. Wright's father was an early day freighter into the Bend country, homesteading in the Cline Falls area. The Wright's first son, Neil, was lost in the Bataan March during World War II. Courtesy of Emma Wright collection

This is one of Bend's first service stations, in conjunction with a grocery store. It was located just after the turn onto Wall Street before reaching Pioneer Park. The billboard gave distances to other towns. There was only one gasoline pump, and water and air were available at the two posts that held up the porch. The date is unknown, possibly around 1920. Pioneer Park was a regular overnight park for travelers, which is no longer true. Courtesy of Madge Smith Glassow collection

The Pine Tavern, at the west end of Oregon Street, overlooking the Deschutes River, is known for its fine food and friendly atmosphere. Fresh out of Oregon Agricultural College (now Oregon State College) in 1919, with home economics degrees, Martha Becher and Maren Gribskov started looking for a location for a restaurant. They got no further than Bend. It was a town of single men working at the mills with few places to eat. Martha and Maren cleaned out a dirty restaurant in Mike Dagic's building on Bond Street across from Aune's Livery Stable, and started cooking on a wood stove. Their customers were mostly bachelors and teachers.

Martha and Maren called their restaurant the OAC for their alma mater, the Oregon Agricultural College. Whenever they attempted to explain the name to their customers, they would nod and say, "Oh, I see." Finally, they stopped trying to explain and changed the name to OIC.

The restaurant outgrew its location, and, since they wanted to attract more customers, the ladies moved it to a new location on Wall Street. They branched out to catering and serving meals to service clubs, then moved again, needing more room. Martha married one of the bachelor loggers, Sid Conklin, and moved to a mill camp. Her sister, Eleanor Becher, came to help Martha and to look after Martha's interest. The restaurant's last move was when the ladies bought a lot on the river from Jim Lawrence and built their Pine Tavern Restaurant. They sold their interest in the restaurant, in 1967, but continued to live in Bend because they liked the people and the weather, summer and winter. Photo from a Pine Tavern menu, story courtesy of Joyce Tifft Gribskov from her book, *Pioneer Spirits of Bend*

Mrs. (Hattie) Mayne's nursing home on Kansas Street filled a long-felt need in 1919. The lumbermen's hospital was primarily for loggers and sawmill workers, though its small x-ray machine was called into use to look at a broken bone in an emergency. But after Mrs. Hall moved to Portland, an expectant mother had no hospital to go to closer than Prineville.

Mrs. Mayne probably washed and diapered more new babies than any woman in Bend before she had to move to larger quarters. Courtesy of Violet Mayne Franks collection

She soon discovered that she needed more room and another nursing home was built on quiet East Third street among the trees and very few homes further out. Courtesy of the Violet Mayne Franks collection

COFFEE
CAFE
BAKERY
BUILDING
MATERIAL
DONT MISS THIS SHOW
FLYING FORTRESS
& VOICE OF TERROR
LIBERTY

Bend seldom has enough snow to talk about, but old-timers still remember the big snow of 1919. Snow was scraped into the center of the street, and business went on as usual under a sunny sky. Even small snows brought out cameras and a round of picture-taking. The signs show a big change of businesses after the "war to end all wars."

Snow usually disappeared under Bend's sunny sky, but the 1919 snow lasted and lasted. Courtesy of Claude Kelley collection

THE ONLY

KNITTING MILL

IN CENTRAL OREGON

If you appreciate the real value of

PURE WORSTED WOOL

in

SWEATERS
SCARFS
COATS
UNDERWEAR, ETC.

Made to Your Measure. Let our agent show you our goods, or write.

THE BEND WOOLEN MILLS

Factory 1850 East First St.

P. O. Box 696 Bend, Oregon

This advertisement was from the *Central Oregon Press* in 1925. Yes, there was a knitting mill in the brick building on the north edge of town. That building housed many different businesses. It was a butcher shop first, after long disuse. The mill that promised so much for Bend just couldn't make it through the Depression and was forced into bankruptcy. But mostly, it was the scene of much dancing, as it is now. The knitting mill was entirely owned by Bend businessmen who saw into the future when there would be no big mills to employ its people. From the author's collection

This shows Newport Bridge during the big snowstorm of 1919. The many new houses seen in the photograph were built after Newport Bridge was built in 1913, crossing the Bend Power and Light Company dam. With the new bridge near town, Newport Avenue, on the brickyard road, began to be settled. Awbrey Road, the first street on the left after crossing the bridge, was a little slower in being built up. Homes of prominent business-people were larger and better with an architect drawing the plans. The A. H. Horns bought the lots on the first street off Awbrey Road, on the right. The Horn house, the new bungalow, two-storied type, was built in 1915 on a knoll, overlooking the river and dam, and with a good view of the mountains. The houses of the George Childs, owner of Bend Hardware; and Bob Huffschmidt, of the new iron works foundry, were built across the street nearer the river, separated close to their outside lines, and one-story, not to interfere with the Horns's view. And, of course, they were built with brick. Cashman, of the Cashman's Men's Wear clothing store built a one-story home on the corner of First Street and Awbrey Road. Charles, ("Chuck") Hunnell, of the Bend Garage, built a house down close to the river, behind the present Elks lodge. The first houses seen in the photograph on the corner of Newport and Awbrey Road were, on the corner, the Richard ("Dick") Minters's brick house; then the Stockman home; Stockman's five and ten cent store; and the Inabnets's home (owners of the Inabnet Ladies' Ready to Wear). Courtesy of Marjorie Smith collection

There was a short and disturbing period during the 1920s when patriotism ran high, and the western arm of the Ku Klux Klansmen were fighting at shadows. Those who had joined the Klan soon came to their senses after a cross was burned on top of Pilot Butte. It was then that they realized whom these unknown people in white robes, with faces covered, were against. Courtesy of Louise (Mrs. Phil) Brogan collection

Edith Wilson assists her husband. From *The Living White House* by the White House Historical Society, 1966

Deschutes County School Superintendent J. Alton Thompson, on his return from a tour of inspection of the schools on the High Desert in December 1920, issued an interesting report. He said that Miss Mary Stauffer, the teacher at Hampton School, was unable to show her register because the wind had blown the schoolhouse door open, and some sheep had eaten the records that had been kept for the past nine years. Those records included the names of all the children who had ever attended school in the district. The sheep, he said, also took care of the perennial problem of textbook disposal.

This is a typical, one-room desert school. Hampton was first called Brookings because the Horace Brookings family took up a homestead across from where the Hamptons took up homesteads. Courtesy of the Deschutes County *Pioneer Gazette*

This is a 1920 picture of E. A. Sather (Bend's first groceryman and the first volunteer fire chief), standing beside the side door of his home on northwest Tumalo Street, one of the first nice homes to be built in Bend. His daughters Inga and Cora still live in this well-kept home. Courtesy of Cora Sather

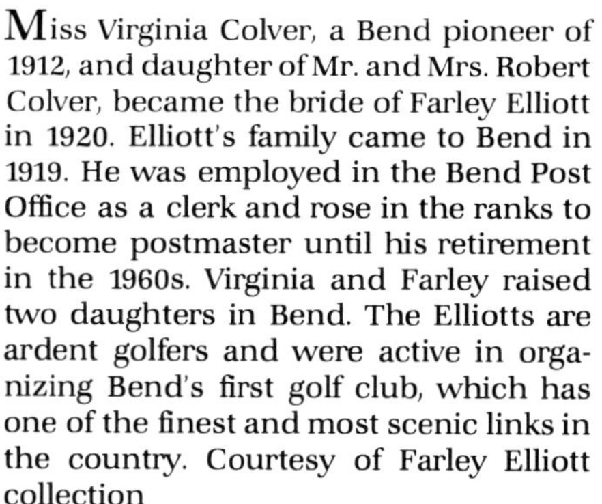

Miss Virginia Colver, a Bend pioneer of 1912, and daughter of Mr. and Mrs. Robert Colver, became the bride of Farley Elliott in 1920. Elliott's family came to Bend in 1919. He was employed in the Bend Post Office as a clerk and rose in the ranks to become postmaster until his retirement in the 1960s. Virginia and Farley raised two daughters in Bend. The Elliotts are ardent golfers and were active in organizing Bend's first golf club, which has one of the finest and most scenic links in the country. Courtesy of Farley Elliott collection

This is a 1922 photograph of Virginia Colver Elliott wearing the latest style in sportswear. The sturdy knickers were a sensible alternative to skirts in this rugged country. The picture was taken at the Cove, now covered by Lake Simtustus in Jefferson County. She was not always as solemn as her wedding picture showed. Courtesy of the Elliott collection

Henry Smith, a visitor to Bend in 1921, found Tumalo State Hatchery interesting. Pearl Lions, the hatchery manager, lived in the cottage behind the gate. This is now Shevlin-Hixon Park, four miles from Bend, past the old brickyard. It is on the other side of the Tumalo Creek as the Smith and Sather timber claims but across the road that runs over the old Indian trail. Courtesy of Madge Smith Glassow collection

This is a photo of the brickyard in 1921. In the lower center is the brickmaking machine, the donkey engine that furnished the steam for running the machinery, and the gasoline pump under a flimsy roof, built to protect men and machinery from the elements but without walls that would keep dust from escaping. Bricks in piles stand in rows to air dry before going to the half-filled kiln. A second kiln has been burned and partly loaded out. Beyond the kilns, out of the picture, is the sawmill. Above the drying brick is the bunkhouse for single men.

Coming off the low hill in the right-hand corner of the picture, the road from Bend divides, and the road above the house continues on to Laidlaw (later changed to Tumalo) and Sisters beyond Tumalo Creek. The other road goes down into the brickyard past the honeymoon house of the author and her husband, Ira Williams. The Horns lived here before moving to town. The road continues on between the barn and the cookhouse to the *little green house*, on the edge of the encroaching clay pit. Built by Barney Lewis, an accomplished artist, it was the only original land claim house in the county to have a coat of paint.

Scattered about the open spaces and in the woods are the houses of the families of men working at the brickyard or sawmill.

The cut-over land on the hill on the extreme right had been covered with timber a short time before. The hill above the Laidlaw road is the west end of Awbrey Butte, changed to Awbrey Heights when fine homes began to climb up its southern slope. From the author's collection

This is spectacular 97-foot Tumalo Falls. It is fifteen miles southwest of Bend on a good road and a short walk through a pine forest past the intake of Bend's water supply. It comes out of the snowfields on Broken Top a short distance away. Courtesy of Violet Mayne Franks collection

As Bend grew and the Deschutes River became clogged with logs from the two big sawmills, Bend went to the mountains to Crane Prairie for its new water source until the summer of 1921. It was fresh and clear at first, then it began to smell and taste bad and many people fell ill. When it was discovered that a poisonous weed was contaminating the water, almost everyone rushed to the brickyard for water.

The gasoline engine, pumping ice cold water from 360 feet down, ran twenty-four hours a day and night while people filled bottles, jugs, barrels, and even water wagons. A policeman was needed to direct the traffic. Everyone in town was drinking brickyard water. Everyone at the brickyard and sawmill drank soda pop made from brickyard water, compliments of the Bend Bottling Works.

This water wagon, brought to Bend sometime before 1917 to keep the dust down around the Brooks-Scanlon sawmill, became a daily visitor at the brickyard, hauling drinking water for the crew.

Years later, when leaks became too numerous to repair, the water wagon was retired to an honored place on the Conley Brooks farm at Mayzata, Minnesota. From Brooks-Scanlon's *Pine Echoes*, December 1954; courtesy of the Rose Hunnel Steidl collection

In the early twenties, even little boys wore modest bathing suits. In front are Hariiet Childs, Eddie Huffschmidt, and Lawrence Jensen. In back is Chester Horn. The children stood in front of Huffschmidt's house on West First Street. From the author's collection

These were teachers at Reid School in 1921. Nell Tifft was principal of Reid School by this time and continued as principal until she married Percy Armstrong in 1926. By this time, she was not only the principal at Reid, but it included the four grades that had spilled over into the Athletic Club gym next door, and another class in the basement of the Lutheran Church. Many of her pupils became well-known Bend businessmen, including Gordon McKay, and Jack and Bob Wettle. Courtesy of Joyce Tifft Gribskov, from the book *Pioneer Spirits of Bend*

Standing in front of the tree is Nell Tifft, one of the teachers at Reid School in January 1921. Nellie Tifft Armstrong began teaching in the Reid School in Bend in 1919. At the end of two years she became principal of the school, a position she retained until she married Percy Armstrong five years later. She is the mother of Joyce Armstrong Gribskov, author of *Pioneer Spirits of Bend.* Courtesy of Joyce Tifft Gribskov, from her book *Pioneer Spirits of Bend*

The second Baptist church, built in 1923, was constructed on the site of the first church, built in Bend and even uses the same bell. Courtesy of Madge Smith Glassow collection

An aerial view of Bend shows the new road going up Pilot Butte, circling around the butte several times to get to the top. This road was made through donations of money from townspeople and business houses in 1922. Aubrey Butte beyond the river has a patch of snow on the northeast side. There is also some leftover snow in the meadow surrounding the brickyard. This small meadow was protected by surrounding hills and timber so the snow lingered there longer than many other places.

The park on top of Pilot butte is called the Tom Foley Park for Bend's first Water, Light, and Power Company manager, the father of Judge Robert Foley. Courtesy of William Van Allen collection

These girls are doing a maypole dance at one of the Fourth of July celebrations. Marjorie Smith is facing the photographer. No one will give the date as it would also reveal their present ages. Courtesy of Marjorie Smith collection

Wetle's, built in 1923 by John Wetle, faces Minnesota Street. Minnesota runs west toward Wall Street, but it doesn't cross Wall because behind Wetle's and across the alley is the river. The department store was destroyed by fire in 1962. Damage to the building and contents ranged into the hundreds of thousands of dollars. Unfortunately, the store was not insured for its full value. With Shevlin-Hixon quitting, Wetle's might have quit, too, but it reopened.

Wetle's second store was bigger and better than ever. New departments were added, doubling its size. Wetle's was the one store on Wall that was continuously owned and run by the same family. (John Wetle died in 1976 at the age of 86.) Tourist trade dropped off when the traffic was diverted to Third Street. Wetle's quit business with a big closing out sale in October 1981, after fifty-eight years in business. Courtesy of the *Bend Bulletin*

These 1927 photographs are of the Wetle children growing up in Bend. Their father, sitting on the running board of their Ford touring car, started the Wetle store at the south end of Minnesota Street on Wall Street. Courtesy of the *Bend Bulletin*

This four-piece band, along with Connie Knickerbocker Amsberry at the piano, made music and quickened steps all over central Oregon in the Roaring Twenties. They played "Lazy River," "Sleepy Time Gal," and hundreds more. The music went on for hours every night, except Sundays. The musicians earned five dollars a night, which they thought was good pay. From left to right in this 1923 photograph are Orville Shultz (violin), Woodson Smith (saxophone), Paul Hosmer (banjo) and Hugh Amsberry (saxophone and banjo). With no television to show them the Charleston and other late steps, young Bend folks were still dancing the Missouri waltz, the two-step, the one-step and the Paul Jones. Courtesy of Anson McCook; from the *Deschutes County Gazette,* January 1976

Bend's fire department building is still on Minnesota Street between Lava Road and Bond Street, but the 1925 (and earlier) equipment has been changed. Courtesy of Dorothy Vandevert collection; photograph from the *Bend Bulletin*

This hunting party expected to get their deer as well as have a good time. Oscar Franks lined his friends up in 1925 and photographed them, from left to right, front row: Harold Hunnell, Violet Mayne Franks, Melvin O'Day. Kneeling in front, Cletes Redmond Hunnell, Alice Carver, Emma McBride Wright, and Leslie Wright. In the back row are James Mayne and Lloyd Mayne. Courtesy of Violet Mayne Franks collection

In the upper right of this picture, dwarfed by the immensity of Paulina Peak, is the lonely Forest Service lookout. It's only a short hike around the edge of the crater to the spot where this picture was taken. College students frequently take summer jobs watching for forest fires from these high points. Courtesy of the *Big Haul*, September 1963

Bend's newly organized Skyliner Club was looking for good skiing areas. Here they are in January 1924, near Windy Point close to the summit of the McKenzie Pass. Not all members could obtain skis so they took turns using the pairs they had. Courtesy of Claude Kelley collection

This is a view of HooDoo Bowl on the summit of Santium Pass a few miles from Bend where many Bend skiers skied until the Bachelor Butte area was made more available for winter sports. A 400-foot double chair lift carried skiers to the top, as seen in the upper left of the picture, and three rope tows took care of the less experienced skiers who preferred a gentler slope. Courtesy of Rose Hunnell Steidl collection; photograph by Jim Hosmer

This U. S. Forest Service tree farm, on the north edge of Bend, is where pines are grown to replace trees on land where many have been cut down. Courtesy of U. S. Forest Service

Bill Tromblee and Minnie Hoover are pictured here in Bill's handmade *bug*, in about 1924. Didn't all young men make their own bugs from secondhand cars? Courtesy of Marjorie Hoover Tromblee collection

This automobile was traveling through McKenzie Pass on May 5, 1928. The road is seldom plowed out before the last of May or the Fourth of July. Courtesy of Marjorie Hoover Tromblee collection

This is a photograph of a sheepshearing crew on the High Desert near Glass Butte in 1928. Several brothers who owned sheep ranches brought their sheep to this location, although the crew usually moved to big ranches. Members of the crew, from left to right: Bart Kelley; Oscar Franks; Tom Wyman; in back, Oat Evans; John Franks; and Emma McBride Wright, cook. The tall man and the men in the back are not remembered. Violet Mayne Franks, another cook, took the picture. Courtesy of Violet Mayne Franks

Note the latest styles of telephones shown in Manheimer's window display in 1928. The Pacific Telephone Company took over from the Deschutes Telephone Company in 1916. The office was on the northwest corner of Franklin Street. There was no phone service through Prineville. The Prineville operator, who was also the postmaster, storekeeper, and stage agent, cut off the phone while he sorted mail, often half a day at a time. Courtesy of Madge Smith Glassow collection

This is the first post office crew to work in the post office on the corner of Wall and Franklin streets, built in 1930. Reading from left to right, front row: I. A. L. Cavaness; Farley Elliott; Willard Higgins; James Gould; Angie Sedgwich; Paul Loree; George Davenport; Ray Allen; and Carl Hatch. Back row: L. B. Baird, postmaster; Samuel Seeds; Tracy Tyler; the building engineer's name is unknown; Jay Noble; Robert Martin, center step with cap; Kenneth Bennett; Vern Smith; Harold Hansen; and Irving Walter. Courtesy of Farley Elliott collection

Main Post Office, on the corner of Wall and Franklin, was built about 1933. A new one that handles the mail on Fourth Street off Revere was built in 1981, but it probably will never replace this one for popularity. Courtesy of Virginia Colver Elliott collection

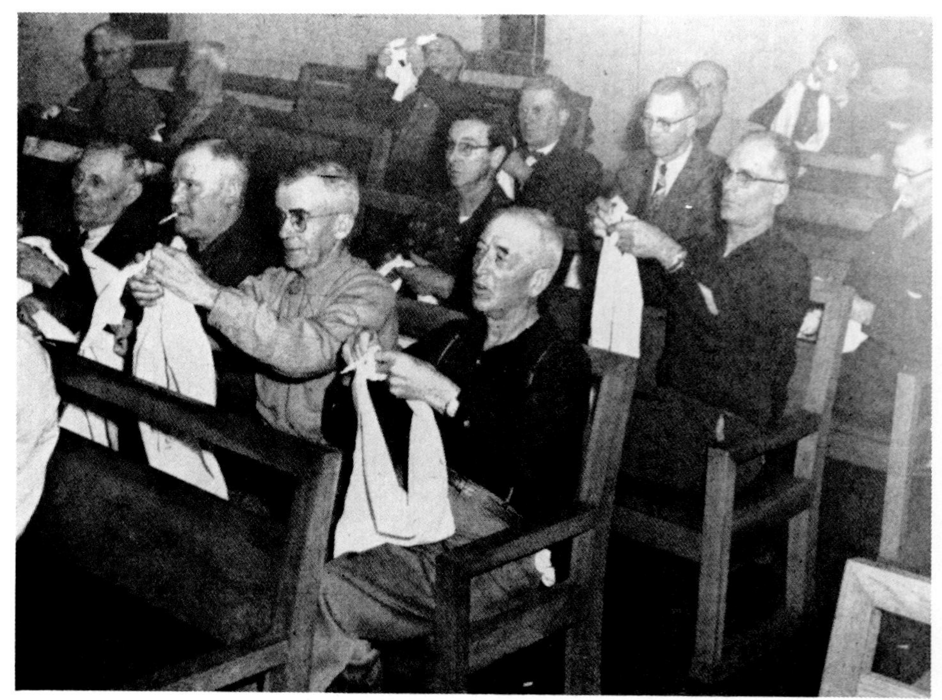

This isn't a home economics class in diaper folding, according to the late Paul Hosmer, long-time editor of Brooks-Scanlon's *Pine Echoes.* These men were sawmill stiffs and lumberjacks getting a lesson in first aid. Meetings were held in the county courthouse and were attended by as many as fifty or sixty men from plants and camps. Several of these men were World War I veterans.

From left to right they were: front row—Oscar Larson, John Steidl, Lyle Gilliland, and George Conklin. Second row—Jack Wanichek and Roy Glassow. Behind them—Arnold Sandwick, Maurice Melsness, and Steve Steidl. Upper rear—Don Williams and Clint Olson. Far left—Jack DeRussia, Bill Officer, and, all tangled up in a towel, Ted Meagher. Courtesy of Paul Hosmer, from the *Pine Echoes,* July 1958; photograph by Web Loy

This Norwegian picnic was the first of many such get-togethers for many of the loggers and millworkers who had followed the big mills from the Dakotas and Minnesota. Some traveled directly from the Old Country. Many of these people, including the Sathers and the N. P. Smiths, followed or preceded the big mills from Minnesota. Courtesy of Cora Sather collection

SUNDAY — REGULAR PRICES

MONDAY — TUESDAY

Pay What You Can!

We want everyone to take advantage of this offer. Accept it, please, in the spirit in which it is given. Come as our guests if you can't afford to pay because you are more than welcome. If you wish to pay something—anything from a penny up will admit you and your entire family.

Everybody Come — You Can — You Should

CAPITOL

Before radios and television in the 1920s and 1930s, B. A. "Dutch" Stover, owner of the Capitol Theatre, brightened the Christmas season for many Bend people with this remarkable advertisement in the *Bend Bulletin* for December 28, 1929. The first movie shown in this theatre was "Tess of the Storm Country," with Mary Pickford starring. Westerns were always the most popular with Bend's young people in the twenties. They were short with news reels run between two films. Bill Hart and his horse were favorites. The hero always got the girl but he never kissed her on stage. That was never done in any of the movies. The piano player watched the movie, adding sound effects to match the action. The dialogue was written rather than spoken so there was always more action than words. The movies were often called "flickers" for good reason.

TRAILWAYS

The Continental Trailways bus system had its small beginning at Bend when fifteen-year-old Myrl Hoover bought his first used Studebaker in 1915. Not until 1929, when he was twenty-eight years old, did he think about starting a regular bus route beyond the Bend area.

His Mount Hood Stages expanded to Pacific Trailways, and finally to Continental Trailways. Bend remained headquarters as long as Myrl Hoover was president of the company. If a passenger is riding Trailways from Salt Lake City, Chicago, or New York to Portland, his bus will have a meal stop at Bend and will finish the trip over scenic Wapineta Cutoff on a well-paved road.

This is a photograph of Bend's first school bus. It was privately owned by the driver, fifteen-year-old Myrl Hoover, the oldest son of George and Mary Hoover. Young Myrl had been driving a taxi for his father when he saw this twelve-passenger used Studebaker for sale and decided he wanted to go into business for himself. Besides driving children to school, he jitneyed Shevlin-Hixon men to work and met the morning and night trains for the Pilot Butte Inn. In between time he delivered wood and hauled various small items. He was also a member of Bend's volunteer fire department. Photograph from *Motor Coach Age;* Courtesy of Pacific Trailways

Maurice Hoover is standing beside his brother Myrl's 1928 Cadillac, the forerunner of the Continental Trailways bus. One morning in 1929, twenty-nine-year-old Myrl was on his way to Portland when he gave a ride to two disgruntled men who had missed their bus at Redmond. Beating the bus by one hour on a shorter, but rougher road, the men persuaded Myrl to make regular trips to Portland over the Wapinita Cutoff by Warm Springs, south of Mount Hood, instead of taking the long, roundabout route that the stage took. He agreed to do it every other day. Courtesy of *Motor Coach Age*

Del Matson, hired to drive the stage on alternate days, his wife, and Myrl Hoover are standing beside the new stretched Lincoln in this 1933 photograph. Courtesy of *Motor Coach Age*

Myrl Hoover and Del Matson are standing beside the first real bus, a yellow coach. Courtesy of *Motor Coach Age*

The Mount Hood Stages' Diamond T's carried freight on their tops. This Diamond T was leaving Bend for Boise, Idaho with boxes of flowers stacked on the roof. Courtesy of *Motor Coach Age*

The luggage and freight went in the back end of Diamond T. Courtesy of *Motor Coach Age*

Beginning in 1931, under the name of Mount Hood Stages, the old Hoover Stages gradually bought up or merged with other Oregon stage lines, running from Portland through Bend and Burns to Salt Lake City. Although they had pooled routes, they retained their own independence with Bend as headquarters. Joining with other routes in 1956, the Pacific Trailways pool ran buses as far as Chicago. Continuing to pool new routes, the Continental Trailways ran nationwide, with Bend still headquarters, and with Myrl Hoover as president.

William Niskanen, who had been secretary, purchased enough stock from Myrl and Maurice Hoover to give him controlling interest in 1959. Since then headquarters have been moved to an eastern city. The Pacific Trailways headquarters remains at Bend, with expanded offices over the Trailways Bus station on Bond Street. Courtesy of *Motor Coach Age*

This is the Trailways station and restaurant on the corner of Bond and Greenwood. From the author's collection

Myrl, George, and Maurice Hoover are shown in 1959, when all Hoover interest in the Trailways was sold to William Niskanen and they retired. Courtesy of Marjorie Hoover Tromblee

Bend's first water pageant was on July Fourth, 1933, the brainchild of a group of Bend businessmen who wanted something different from Bend's usual parade through the streets. Mirror Pond became the setting with Drake Park's slope to the water's edge furnishing lots of seating space. The floats increased in beauty during the years as the pageant's fame spread, drawing crowds up to 10,000 people who finally spread across the river to sit on private lawns.

From a single float for the young queen and her retinue, later queens rode on the backs of beautiful white swans with their retinues following on more swans much larger than the real ones that make their home on Mirror Pond. The lighted arch also was a later innovation. With a backdrop of snowcapped mountains, at dusk the lighted floats came through the arch. They waited to be turned by the slowed flow of the river to first face the audience and then float past to disappear in the darkness before reaching the dam and Newport Bridge. Each sponsor of a float tried to outdo the others in following the theme.

The water parade was suspended during World War II, and once or twice during other wars. The pageant and holiday festivities in the park came to a sudden halt when the park was invaded by a large group of nudists. There were too many for the local police force to evict. All they could do was send youthful onlookers away. The residents on Drake Road across the river are not eager to have another pageant after the few interrupted years since it was no small job to clean up after their messy uninvited guests. Since tourism has become one of Bend's most important industries, something might be done to solve the problem so this most unique show can be resumed. Courtesy of William Van Allen collection

The 1950 water pageant queen and her retinue floated on their individual swan boats leading the parade through the lighted arch on Mirror Pond. Courtesy of *Bend Bulletin*

From Drake Park the water pageant swans could be seen on Mirror Pond with houses and trees on Pinecrest Drive in the background. Courtesy of William Van Allen collection

The old hay rack and wagon wheels are where they were left on the old Vandevert homestead. The old barn in the background is next to a modern building that is currently in use. Courtesy of Dorothy Vandevert collection

These were the daughters of a man named Chaviss who was working on the railroad at Crescent. They flew into the Redmond airfield on this four-seated charter prop plane in the early thirties. Courtesy of Violet Mayne Franks collection

President Franklin D. Roosevelt signs the Social Security Act, August 14, 1935. Courtesy of Wide World

Bend people were not willing to give up their day parade on the streets for a night performance for the first few years when the pageant was only a few poorly lit floats. The Warm Springs Indians in their feathers and beads always drew a good crowd. They led this 1935 Fourth of July parade. Courtesy of James Arbow collection

This Fourth of July, 1940 parade of progress is proof that horses had not been entirely replaced by cars in this far western town. Notice the lassos tied to the western-style saddles and that the people turned out en masse to see good horseflesh, whether thoroughbred or just off the range. Courtesy of the James Arbow collection

People turned out for a parade, even with snow on the ground. This 1940 parade must have been for something special to bring the Indians up from the Warm Springs Reservation. This view looks north on Wall Street. Courtesy of James Arbow

VIII

1933-1950

Happy days are here again," everyone was singing all over the country after Franklin Delano Roosevelt took office in March 1933 and announced his New Deal. Times had worsened during the months since his election in November 1932. Families were losing their homes, renters were being evicted when rent was unpaid, and farmers were losing their farms. Banks closed all over the country. The First National Bank in Bend closed its doors and its president packed up his belongings and left the state. Men, women, and young boys and girls were riding freight trains sent from town to town, because no one wanted to assume the feeding of so many homeless.

When Roosevelt took office people were lininig up in front of closed doors of banks, demanding their moneY. The stock market on Wall Street in New York closed its doors, and many men lost fortunes and committed suicide.

Two days after Roosevelt assumed the office of president, he declared a bank holiday. All banks were closed until the Department of the Treasury could audit their books. Those that were solvent were supplied with cash for those who still wanted to withdraw their money. The others were closed forever. Knowing their money would be safe, the people stopped the run on the banks. On March 9, Congress was called into special session and turned out the many new laws that Roosevelt asked for in the next ninety-nine days. The NIRA, WPA, AAA, NRA, and CCC all were designed to put men to work. Three CCC (Civilian Conservation Corps) camps were set up in Deschutes County. Boys who had never seen a potato grow, or been in the woods, grubbed brush and built picnic tables for new parks. They cleaned out trails to the Bend country's many lakes, and they were invited into Bend homes and married Bend girls. Many successful businessmen in Bend came with the CCC.

The CWA (Civil Works Administration) supplied hundreds of millions of dollars to cities and states to set up their own public projects. Many businessmen were complaining because the government was spending more than it was collecting in taxes, but everyone was working who was able to work. Veterans hospitals were being built to take care of veterans who were disabled during the war.

The Volstead Act was repealed, and liquor no longer needed to be poured from flasks hidden from sight, and Congress passed the Social Security Act.

Bend celebrated good times on the Fourth of July, 1933, with a water parade on Mirror Pond. The few floats had trouble with their lights, but in the years that followed floats and lighting improved, with up to 10,000 people coming from great distances to sit on the sloping lawn of Drake Park and watch this unique spectacle. Mrs. Mayne moved her hospital to a new home on dusty East Third Street where there were few homes. Within a few decades this street becme a through-state highway, taking traffic away from downtown. It became lined with gas stations, motels, quick food restaurants, and five big shopping centers, for Bend was becoming a mecca for fishermen in the summer and skiers in the winter. Many liked the all-around weather, with 365 days of sunshine, and decided to stay.

Roosevelt had an easy victory in 1936. Hitler, Mussolini, and Tojo were rattling machine guns and moving in on weaker nations. Bend people were divided, as was Congress, when Roosevelt wanted to strengthen the army and navy. Congress passed laws to keep America free of foreign entanglements. Many people didn't think the situation was as dangerous as Roosevelt believed. Roosevelt demanded that Japan apologize and pay for sinking the United States gunboat *Panay*. It complied.

Roosevelt ran and became president for the third time in 1940, and Congress passed a law that a president should take office in January, following the election, instead of having a "lame duck" president and Congress passing and vetoing laws for two more months.

Deschutes County courthouse, in Bend's first high school building, was gutted by fire, burning all property records, with names and dates of early transactions, as well as the late ones someone was trying to destroy. There was a scramble for birth certificates when Congress passed the Selective Service (or draft) Act in September 1940, when all men between eighteen and forty-five were required to register. The state capitol, the only place with duplicate records, also burned about this time. Bibles were produced, and doctors and friends who knew of birthdates were asked to sign certificates. Historians were hard pressed to learn first names and initials of early settlers. It is better to leave such information out, rather than to depend on fading memories and have misinformation repeated as truth.

Few people were living in the past in 1940. A whole new world had opened up with radio. Those first crystal sets with wire strung all over the house and attic rafters to bring in the faintest music had given way to table sets and cabinet sets that could pass as phonographs. Almost everyone listened to *Amos and Andy* and the scratchy music of Tommy Dorsey. They saw the New Year out with Guy Lombardo and his band. They didn't need to see faces; they could tell one voice from another. It was a listening audience, not a watching one.

December 7, 1941 was the day of infamy. The Japanese bombed Pearl Harbor.

It was a Sunday morning. Many people were listening to a ball game on their radio when the President's voice broke in. There was disbelief. A Japanese envoy was in Washington, D.C., talking peace. People called relatives, friends, asking if they had been listening. "The Japs are bombing Pearl Harbor." Pearl Harbor in Hawaii had seemed far away until that morning, and then it seemed to be on everyone's doorstep. The telephone lines were swamped with people trying to get through to relatives over there, wanting to know if they were all right.

Recruiting stations opened up for men clamoring to kill the Japs. Women who were free from family cares wished there was something they could do besides stay at home and wrap bandages. They would be given their chance a year later when the Women's Auxiliary Army Corp (WAAC) was opened for enlistments. But they were just an auxiliary. They took jobs that could be done behind the lines. That year, they proved that they could be good soldiers. They were given the privilege of leaving the WAAC and going home, or enlisting in the regular Women's Army Corps (WAC). Most of them stayed. Gradually, the Navy, the Air Force, the Marines, and the Coast Guard were enlisting women.

General Agee flew into the Redmond Airfield to tell about the new filter center being constructed in Bend for the Ground Observation Corps. If the Japanese were audacious enough to attack Pearl Harbor, they might well attempt landing on the long, unfortified coast of Oregon. Civilians were given a course on airplane identification before manning observation posts around the clock on high points around Bend, until radar was set up on the coast to pick up enemy planes out at sea. A fire had been set on Oregon's coast, and a Japanese bomb had killed a woman and child in a park near Klamath Falls.

The blackout on the Oregon coast and in the Willamette valley was not imposed on the area east of the Cascades, but Bend had to be prepared to accept civilian evacuees if the Japanese should attempt to land on the coast. A thousand men and women were recruited to work in the ordinance plant the government built in Bend where service jeeps, cars, and trucks were repaired and put back into commission.

Camp Abbott was built on the Big Meadow and took over the Bend-Redmond airfield. The Army Corps of Engineers insignia wearers became more numerous on Bend streets than local residents. Bend women used their butter and sugar rations to make pies, cakes and cookies to take to the U.S.O. and stayed to talk and dance with the service people away from home.

Then suddenly, Camp Abbott was moved to Tacoma, leaving only the recently completed officers club building. Hunters were allowed to hunt for game on the High Desert where they had been excluded during the maneuvers of the 153rd engineers.

"The President is dead." President Roosevelt died at Warm Springs, Arkansas, and Harry ("Give 'em hell") Truman was president. The atom bomb, in the process of being tested for the past five years, was ready to be used, a decision that he shared with the other Allied leaders. The Japanese were scattered over many islands. Twice United States planes flew over Japan bombing defense plants. Then an atomic bomb was dropped on Nagasaki with a warning that Tokyo would be next brought a quick plea for peace and the end of the war. Bend celebrated V-J day with a parade. And in 1946, Bend's Fourth of July water pageant was bigger and better than ever, drawing over 10,000 people watching from the riverbank of Drake Park, and a crowd overflowing onto lawns across the river, leaving garbage for homeowners to clean up.

Percy Stevens American Legion Post No. 4 changed its name to Stevens-Chute Post, honoring Bend's first casualty in World War II. The post opened its membership to the new veterans with honorable discharges.

The World War veterans knew what it was to come home with no money to buy homes, the farm of their dreams or a business, or to return to school. From every post in the country came resolutions that were worked over and consolidated with resolutions from the other veterans' organizations. From them came the Serviceman's Readjustment Act, better known as the G.I. (General Issue) Bill. They already had veterans hospitals, gained after a long struggle. These veterans' benefits were extended to the veterans of the Korean and Vietnam conflicts, as were invitations for these new veterans to join the different veterans' organizations started after World War I.

The Shevelin-Hixon Lumber Company had cut all its timber and there was not enough government timber to keep two mills running, so it sold its interest to Brooke-Scanlon after thirty-four years of operation in Bend. Shevelin-Hixon cut its last log in December 1950. At that time they had 850 men employed, 625 at the mill and 225 in the woods. Only three of the original buildings were not demolished. These were approved on the National Register of Historic Sites. They are being used by different small nonpolluting manufacturing plants.

This photograph was taken in 1937 in front of Ernest Smith's electric shop before he moved to Wall Street. In the photograph are: Madge Smith Glassow; Bruce Markell; E. A. Smith; and Homer Smith, Madge's brother. Courtesy of Madge Smith Glassow collection

Father Luke Sheehan's funeral was said to have been the biggest ever seen in Bend up to that time, February 13, 1937. Coming to Bend in 1910 from his native Cork, Ireland, he covered over 8,600 square miles, ministering to his flock in central Oregon. This second Catholic church was built in 1921-22, taking the place of the first one on Wall Street. Courtesy of James Arbow collection

This is one of the Bend boys who answered his country's call in World War II. James (Jimmy) Wright, son of Emma Wright, served on the U.S.S Farragut. Courtesy of Violet Mayne Franks

During World War II, Camp Abbot had a brief life on the Big Meadow from May 1943 to June 1944. Named for the brilliant army engineer, Henry Larcom Abbot, who had camped on the meadow in 1855, the camp became the home of more than 75,000 members of the 153rd Engineers who fought over and flew over 10,000 square miles of desert country during their military maneuvers. The area was closed to deer hunters. The Engineer gate was made from peeled lodgepole pine logs. Mount Bachelor can be seen a few miles in the distance. Drawing by Lloyd A. Allen. Courtesy of Gladys Mayne McFall collection

Colonel Frank S. Besson was commander of Camp Abbot Engineer Replacement Training Camp from 1943 to 1944. Courtesy of William Van Allen and the Oregon Historical Society

In World War II these olive green field tents lined a temporary sagebrush street on the High Desert during early fall maneuvers of the army engineers. Hunters were excluded from the area and wild game sought a safer place to browse. This area once had a homestead house on every 360 acres, but they had all disappeared many years before the army moved in. Courtesy of the *Deschutes Pioneer Association Gazette*; photograph by Norman V. Snyder

These women are only four out of many Bend men and women who worked at the ordinance plant in Bend. They were in the sorting department making up parts needed to repair government cars, trucks, and jeeps during World War II. Expert repairmen worked in the repair shop. From left to right they were: a woman remembered only as Billy; June Kissler; Violet Franks; and Maxine Woods. Courtesy of Violet Mayne Franks collection

Anyone spending any time in Camp Abbot's hospital will remember the smiling face of volunteer nurse Dorothy Vandevert. She went on to become the Pioneer Association Queen in 1975. Courtesy of Dorothy Vandevert collection; photograph by Webb Loy

This building on Wall Street between Minnesota and Franklin streets, that now houses a paint store, served as Bend's U.S.O. during the time that Camp Abbot was on Big Meadow. There were always food and music, and women to talk and dance with the servicepeople in their midst. Many Bend homes were also open to guests from camp. From the author's collection

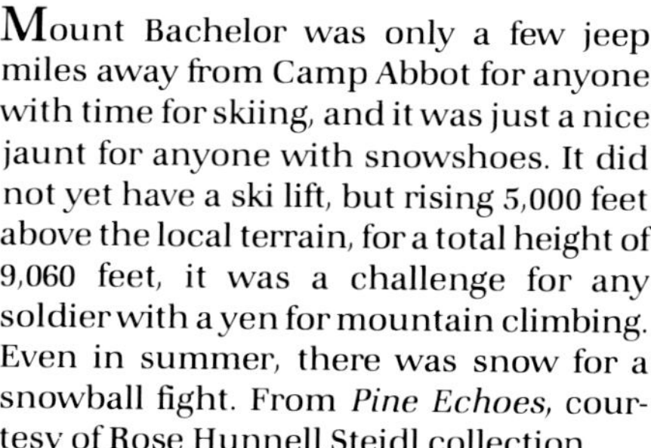
Mount Bachelor was only a few jeep miles away from Camp Abbot for anyone with time for skiing, and it was just a nice jaunt for anyone with snowshoes. It did not yet have a ski lift, but rising 5,000 feet above the local terrain, for a total height of 9,060 feet, it was a challenge for any soldier with a yen for mountain climbing. Even in summer, there was snow for a snowball fight. From *Pine Echoes*, courtesy of Rose Hunnell Steidl collection

These heavy bodied chucker partridges were planted in the Bend country in the 1940s, a fine game bird addition to the almost depleted sage hens. Courtesy of the *Bend Bulletin*

This is Sunriver Lodge south of Bend as it looked in 1981, with additions to the original officers club built while Camp Abbot occupied Big Meadow during World War II. The servicemen who worked on the rustic building during freezing weather had barely thawed out their fingers before Camp Abbot was moved to Fort Lewis in Washington, leaving only the newly completed officers club. Only one dance was held with young ladies from Bend brought out in a bus to dance with the officers at the club.

Sunriver Properties, Inc. bought Big Meadow from the government, and it is now a beautiful resort community with many beautiful summer houses as well as permanent residences. Courtesy of Sunriver Properties, Inc.

Bend's float in Portland's Rose Festival parade in 1946 carried four lovely ladies. Courtesy of Virginia Colver Elliott collection

Ever since they were invented we have wanted to get a picture of a jet plane taking off and we had our chance this month when a fast little bullet of a plane flew into Redmond air field to bring General Agee to Bend for a speech telling us about the new filter center for the Ground Observation Corps now under construction in Bend. The above picture is as close as "we came to it." This picture and caption were in the March 1955 issue of Brooks-Scanlon's *Pine Echoes*. Courtesy of Rose Hunnell Steidl

"Ever since they were invented we have wanted to get a picture of a jet plane taking off and we had our chance this month when a fast little bullet of a plane flew into Redmond air field to bring General Agee to Bend for a speech telling us about the new filter center for the Ground Observation Corps now under construction in Bend. The above picture is as close as we came to it." Courtesy of Brooks-Scanlon's *Pine Echoes*

This shows Bend's City Hall in the old *Bend Bulletin* building on Wall Street. From the author's collection

"Daddy" Lloyd Mayne, a World War II veteran, takes his daughter, Margaret, to Drake Park to meet the Canadian geese about 1949. A few pieces of bread entice the geese out of Mirror Pond. The two-story white house in the background on Broadway and Louisiana streets is the home of James Mayne, the former owner of the Congress Grocery. Courtesy of Violet Mayne Franks collection

Here, sandhill cranes are engaged in their fantastic dance. The cranes are now on the endangered species list. Courtesy of the Oregon Game Commission

IX

1950-1970

Hollywood, and the National Aeronautics and Space Administration (NASA), discovered the Bend country in the late 1960s. Bend celebrated Oregon's centennial in 1959. And Dwight (Ike) Eisenhower, while running for president in 1952, promised to visit Korea and end the Korean conflict, an undeclared war. As president he sent advisers to Vietnam, the site of the longest and most controversial war in United States history, another undeclared war, with America furnishing more fighting men and money than all the other participating United Nations combined.

John F. Kennedy, the first Catholic president, was shot down in Dallas, Texas. His brother, Robert Kennedy, was also killed when running for president. The country was rocked a third time when Martin Luther King was shot when he was telling his people they could overcome centuries of discrimination by peaceful sitdown strikes.

Expecting to land on the moon, NASA sent Neil Armstrong to Bend's Moon Country to try out a bulky white spacesuit on more rugged terrain than they expected to find on the moon. From Pine Mountain observatory came the last televised photographs of Apollo 11 leaving the earth's atmosphere and again the first pictures of its reentry.

Classes at Bend's Union High School were double shifting when the Bend people decided they needed a junior or community college with evening classes held in the high school. With a donation of land on Awbrey Butte, this developed into a fully accredited Central Oregon Community College.

With 360 days of sunshine, Bend was one of the first communities with houses heated with solar heat. Every morning, winter and summer, Bend folks can look up and see seven snowcapped mountains, the lowest one towering 7,802 feet into the sky and dwarfed by 10,354-foot South Sister. Bachelor Butte is the seventh in the row of high peaks. (Many wonder why this 9,060-foot mountain was ever called a butte!) Standing off by itself away from the three beautiful sisters, first called Hope, Faith, and Charity, it was a bachelor indeed.

This maze of three 500-foot deep canyons where the fast-flowing Deschutes, Metolious, and Crooked rivers meet, shut out early pioneering traffic from the north. Two hydroelectric power dams, Pelton and Round Top, have backed up the water from these three rivers, forming Billy Chinook and Simtustus lakes. The lakes cover Opal Springs and the Cove, two spots remembered fondly by old-timers, but the lakes are a delight for fishermen on rafts and motorboats.

Simtustus was chief of the Warm Springs Indians, and, with Billy Chinook, he signed the treaty of 1855. After signing the treaty they went peacefully to the Warm Springs Reservation, of which the chief said, before signing, "I have never been there, but if it was any good white men would have it." Several small family groups were merged into the Warm Springs tribe. The Piutes, horse Indians from eastern Oregon, had never been friendly with the fish eaters that had gone to Warm Springs Reservation and returned to their own pleasant warm springs and lake area, taking their horses with them. The Warm Springs Indians, who coveted the horses, called the Piutes "horse thieves," and the army had another excuse for fighting the Piutes. Courtesy of the Oregon State Highway Department

These Lava Bears from Bend's Union High School carry on the tradition of pioneers, "if you want anything done, do it yourself." Here they are building their own float on Wall Street for the 1953 Fourth of July parade. Courtesy of William Van Allen collection

Myrtle Sheperd Thompson receives a bouquet of red roses and congratulations from Edna Boyd Brinson, Deschutes Pioneer Association president, upon being chosen 1951 pioneer queen. Also in the photograph are pioneers Kenneth Sawyer, editor of the *Bend Bulletin*, and Claudia Triplett Martin, secretary. Courtesy of Carol Boyd collection

This 1959 photograph shows the first six presidents of the Deschutes Pioneer Association, organized in 1946, who got this fine organization off to a good start. Reading from left to right with the dates of their arrivals in the Bend country: William Burton, 1906; Claude Vandevert, born in the Powell Butte district near Bend in 1891; LeRoy Fox, 1909; Edna Boyd Brinson, 1905; Earnest Smith, 1904 or 1905; and Carl Johnson, date of arrival unknown. Courtesy of Carol Boyd collection

These members of the Deschutes Pioneer Association went back to school for their Oregon Centennial celebration in January, 1959. Reading from left to right, front row: Cecil Hollinshead, Francis Steidl, Claudia Triplett Martin, Edna Boyd Brinson, Ivan McGillvary, Ruth Caldwell Coyner, and Claude Vandevert, who brought his mouse to school. Second row, left to right: Clarence Boyd trying to hook Francis's lunch box; Steve Steidl; Ann Linster Weaver; Flossie Reed Smith; Mary Hoover, taking the part of a mother visiting the school with her baby; Earnest Smith; and Marian West Coe, who attended school at Bend but was acting teacher in this photograph. Courtesy of Carol Boyd collection

Celebrating Oregon's centennial year in 1959, at the winter meeting in January of the Deschutes Pioneer Association, these pioneers searched in old trunks for clothes of yesteryear that they were still able to wear. Reading from left to right, with the years of their arrival in the Bend country: John Steidl, 1902; Francis Steidl Jackson, 1902; Lilly Hollinshead, 1924; Dorothy Vandevert, 1927; Marium Triplett Hoover, 1909. Second row, left to right: Mrs. H. C. Ellis, 1905; Edna Boyd Brinson, 1905; Janett Keys Stollmack, 1912; Claudia Triplett Martin, 1902; the next woman is not recognized; Addie Triplett; Flossie Reed Smith, 1904; Earnest Smith, 1905. Back row: Dean Hollinshead, 1898; Carl Johnson, date unknown. Courtesy of Carol Boyd collection

State Representative Sam Johnson flew into Redmond in 1951 on the first flight of one of the larger airplanes. Johnson was the president of the Deschutes Pioneer Association in 1979. Courtesy of *Bend Bulletin*

Roberts Field, midway between Redmond and Bend, was named to honor John Roy Roberts, a Redmond pioneer and merchant in the early 1900s. He is honored for his untiring efforts to bring big planes to the area. Roberts was a member of the Redmond Airport Commission from its beginning. For several years he was on the Oregon State Board of Aeronautics, and for one year was its chairman. He was named "Mr. Aeronautics of Oregon" at a celebration in Redmond in 1965. He died June 15, 1970, at the age of eighty-eight, his long-time dream realized, but after he was too old for flying lessons and a pilot's license.

Almost as soon as Roberts Field was opened, the government took it over during World War II, returning it at the end of the war. Courtesy of *Bend Bulletin*, August 7, 1981

The front side of Fort Benham, named for the falls nearby, is protection from the Indians. Courtesy of Rose Hunnel Steidl collection; photograph from the Brooks-Scanlon *Pine Echoes*

Hollywood found the Bend country in the late fifties, and that was only the beginning. A fort was never built so fast or easily in the Hudson's Bay Company trapping days. With modern machinery and power tools, Fort Benham was ready for the first influx of movie people within days. Courtesy of *Pine Echoes*; photograph by William Allen

Actors practice a scene with local people as extras in *Town of Bitter, Day of the Outlaw,* the first of a number of productions filmed in the Benham Falls, Mount Bachelor area.

The Way West, a Pulitzer Prize winner, was also filmed in the Bend country, in 1966. Harold Hecht (the producer), Kirk Douglas, Robert Mitchum, Richard Widmark, and Lola Albright stayed at the Pilot Butte Inn during production. Their Chimney Rock came right out of the Bend country at Fort Rock. Courtesy of Rose Hunnell Steidl collection; from the Brooks-Scanlon *Pine Echoes*

Burl Ives wanted a blizzard for his movie *The Indian Fighter,* filmed at Bend's Fort Benham, but he got more than he asked for in the big snow the winter of 1958. The stockade is in the background of this picture. Ives stayed warm in the Pilot Butte Inn. From Books-Scanlon's *Pine Echoes,* courtesy of Rose Hunnell Steidl

Governor Mark Hatfield, later a United States senator from Oregon, rode in a Christmas parade in Bend in 1960. Bend has never put up a podium or parade stand. Important guests either rode in the parade or stood on the sidewalk to watch along with the other onlookers. Courtesy of William Van Allen collection

This tree, the largest Ponderosa pine in Oregon, was slated for demolition because old trees harbor pine beetles. Located on the bank of the Deschutes River about twenty miles south of Bend, it is estimated to be about 500 years old. With a diameter of eight and a half feet at four and a half feet above ground, it is approximately 160 feet high. It has not been cut down. Phil Brogan, former editor of the *Bend Bulletin*, is showing the size of the tree in comparison with a large man. Courtesy of the *Big Haul*, September 1963

The Department of Oregon American Legion held their parade down well-paved Wall Street during their convention in Bend in 1962. This was Bend's first time to host any convention. Courtesy of William Van Allen collection

The man in this photograph is astronaut Walter Cunningham, on the pumice fields near McKenzie Pass in May, 1967, testing a prototype of the suit he would be wearing in the upcoming moon exploration. NASA discovered that Moon Country near Bend had all the features they expected to find on the moon and was better than their lunar surface simulated area at Houston.

Fifteen to twenty feet of soft pumice, volcanic ash, sharp lava, and volcanic glass piled loosely on steep hillsides, as well as lava caves and tubes, tested man's ability to walk in a heavy suit and tested the suit's ability to hold up under expected land conditions on the moon.

Observers on Pine Mountain, thirty miles south of Bend, were the first to spot and videotape Apollo 14, only five hours after its launching on January 31, 1971, and were the last to lose it six and one half hours later as it disappeared over the horizon. They watched with the naked eye as the spaceship dumped extra fuel that spread like a glowing halo.

With borrowed equipment the six excited young University of Portland students had rushed to the observatory on snowmobiles while the astronauts were getting ready to leave the earth. They were again the first to see the spacecraft on February 7 and videotape the events before any other observatory picked it up. But radio and television stations already knew about Pine Mountain's clear air, for only a couple of months earlier a new white dwarf star had been discovered with the twenty-four inch telescope. Courtesy of League of Women Voters booklet, May 1967

Triple shifting started at Bend's Union High School in 1955 when Central Oregon Community College began evening classes in this high school building. At first it was a vocational school, but it soon began to teach academic courses.

The Oregon Community College Foundation is a nonprofit charitable organization whose purpose is to promote and foster private voluntary support for student aid, educational programs, equipment, and capital needs of the college for students who don't want to or cannot afford to attend the state-supported schools that are all west of the Cascades.

Bend's was the first such organization among Oregon's community colleges and the only one in central Oregon that has survived. At first, four instructors commuted between Klamath Falls and Bend but Klamath Falls no longer exists.

One hundred and seven students enrolled at Bend the first term; twenty-seven of these were full-time students. Courtesy of the *Bend Bulletin*

The new Union High School, built in 1949, filled the north side of Louisiana Street between Bond and Wall streets. By 1955 it was too small, and junior high school classes began meeting in the mornings, with senior high school in the afternoons.

Triple shifting began the same year with the first classes attending the Central Oregon Community College meeting in the school in the evenings.

The name of this school was changed to Cascade Junior High School when the new Bend High School was built on the north slope of Pilot Butte. Courtesy of the Marjorie Smith collection

This photo shows the beginning of construction on the Central Oregon Community College on Awbrey Butte in 1962, with a panorama of mountains in the background. Courtesy of the Central Oregon Community College

This is an aerial view of Central Oregon Community College taken in 1981. The college became a fully accredited two-year college in 1967. The 1979-80 credit enrollment was 21,126 students. Of this number 3,500 were taking educational courses. One hundred and sixty-one veterans attended Central Oregon Community College in 1981. The school has no tax base, so each year it must secure voter approval for the following academic year. This has always passed. Courtesy of the Central Oregon Community College

The library at Central Oregon Community College serves Bend's academic community. Courtesy of Central Oregon Community College

The Demic house on Newport, built in 1936, teems with action and enthusiasm on school days. The community-based and supported Tamarack Learning Center takes only students who are at least two years behind in math, spelling, or reading and leads them into activities using these skills. Half of each day is spent in the classroom, and the other half is spent in private and family counseling conducted by a professional staff. The center is headed by Tom Del Nero, who moved to Bend from Klamath Falls in 1952. He attended Bend area schools—Kingston, Kenwood, Bend Junior High—and graduated from Bend Senior High in 1963. He went on to earn his Ph.D. in psychology before starting the Tamarack Learning Center in 1976. Many of the young people who "caught up" here are enrolled at Central Oregon Community College. Photograph by Thomas Del Nero

Tamarack students restore pioneer cemeteries and research the histories of persons buried in unmarked graves. Another important student project is cutting and delivering wood to senior citizens, and through this activity, conducted during the students' half-day work-learning sessions, they haved learned how to measure material and keep books. Courtesy of *Old Times*, published by the students

Tamarack Students Restore Pioneer Cemeteries

By Manuel Romero

The students of Tamarack are restoring Masten Cemetery in order to preserve Central Oregon's history.The students are repairing existing fences and constructing new fences where needed around the grave site.There is also an on-going classroom project where the students are doing research into the lives of these pioneers,and are attempting to determine the names of the people in the unmarked graves.Similar work is also going to be undergone in Breece and Allen Cemeteries. Information is being obtained by interviewing relatives and friends of the deceased and valuable information is being gathered by going through old newspapers and books. at the Historical Center,C.O.C.C.,and County libraries.

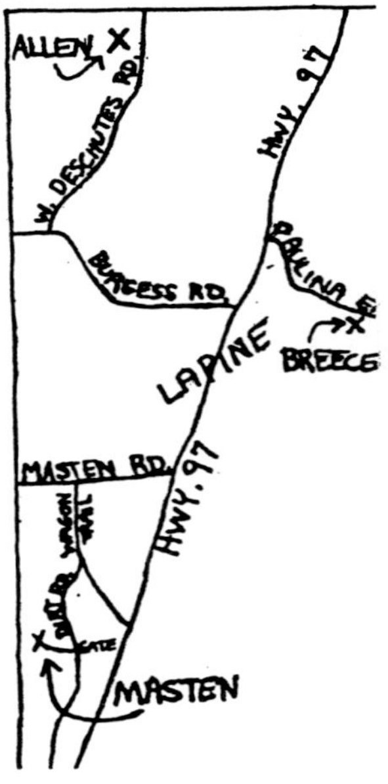

Youth Conservation Corps workers erecting a sign at a bridge they built. The bridge and the trail the workers cleared made hiking easier from Todd Lake to Broken Top. This is just one of the many projects completed under the government youth program that is directed by Arlie Holm, recreation officer for the Bend district of the Deschutes National Forest. Courtesy of *Bend Bulletin*, September 1981

Petersen's Rock Garden draws visitors from throughout the United States, and many Europeans also sign the guest book. A monument to the love of nature and to the industry of Rasmus Petersen, a Danish immigrant who came to central Oregon in 1906, it is a rockhound's delight.

By 1940 Petersen gave up farming to devote full time to turning local rocks into fantastic shapes. He built terraces as well as small buildings surrounded by moats filled with water lilies. He died in his garden in 1952, leaving his work to be watched over by relatives. A small contribution box on a petrified wood stump helps to keep the garden neat and fertile. It is open to the public 365 days a year between 7 a.m. and 9 p.m. Photographs courtesy of Petersen's Rock Garden

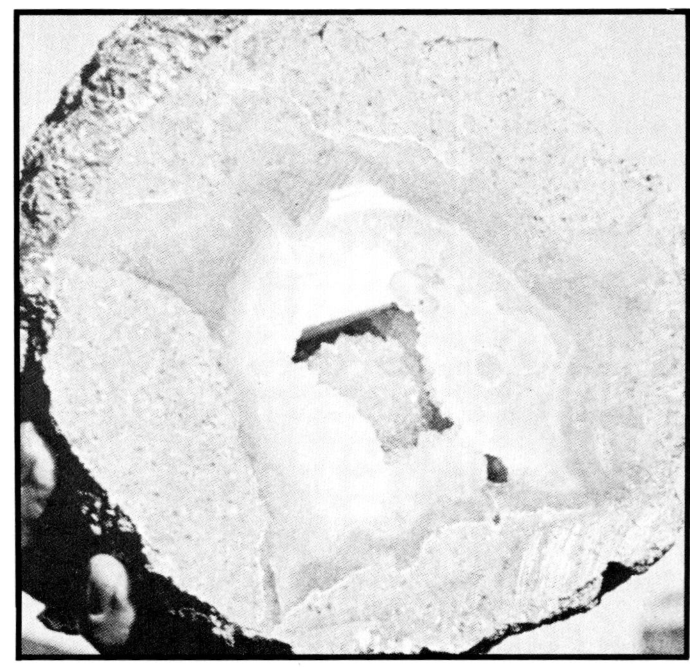

This is the agatized cut center of a thunderegg, Oregon's state rock. Thunderegg is the Indian name for the many dirty-grey rock-encrusted lava balls found in the vicinity of the cinder cones scattered along the southern edge of the High Desert. It is reasonable to believe that some ancestors of the present Indians observed and heard these bomb-like missiles shooting out of a spouting eruption and associated them with thunder.

Experienced rockhounds can tell which of these balls are hollow and which are filled with crystals by hefting them. The action of water on the various salts and iron oxide in the lava inside the balls makes interesting pictures with only a little imagination. Even when nature and water have not completely filled the ball with crystals, leaving a hollow crystallized ball, it becomes an interesting work of art when cut in half. Courtesy of Petersen's Rock Garden

This mounted elk on the roof of the Elks Lodge gives newcomers a start as they drive onto the west ramp of the Newport Bridge. The elk is a large stuffed animal that looks real until one realizes a live elk would not be overlooking the traffic so calmly, even if he had been able to get up there in the first place. Courtesy of Bend Elks Lodge No. 1371

Santa Claus (Sparky Merrill) is at work training a new Rudolph to lead one of many teams that enter parades in towns as far away as Honolulu. He started with only sixteen reindeer from Alaska in 1950. Operation Santa Claus, Inc., located between Bend and Redmond, has grown to the point that as many as sixteen deer are born there each year. It has become the largest commercial reindeer ranch in the United States. Courtesy of Santa Claus, Inc.

The Deschutes County Public Free Library is on the corner of Wall Street and Idaho Avenue. After a number of moves since its beginning in an early *Bend Bulletin* building, the Baptist church annex, and back rooms in the First National Bank Building, the library now has a permanent home that is rapidly becoming outgrown. Courtesy of the Deschutes County Free Public Library

These youngsters are one of the many groups who enjoy the public library facilities. Courtesy of the Deschutes County Free Public Library collection; photograph by the *Bend Bulletin* staff

This photograph was taken in May of 1973 or 1974 from the top of Pilot Butte. It shows patches of snow after a quick cooling of weather that dropped rain west of the mountains and snow on the higher levels. Reading from right to left are the Three Sisters, North Sister, Middle Sister, and South Sister. Hugging South Sister is Broken Top. The next tall mountain is now called Mount Bachelor but oldtimers still refer to it as Bachelor Butte—the one bachelor with the three sisters. The long lower hill on the extreme right is Aubrey Heights, formerly Aubrey Butte, named for an early-day rancher who had the first spread west of the river.

The Deschutes River is hidden behind the fringe of trees and the long, light-colored shed of Brooks sawmill. The road coming around the butte from the left is Greenwood. Some late maps call it a street, but it has always been called just Greenwood. The railroad trestle crosses Greenwood three blocks past busy Third Street. The old part of town runs parallel just east of the trees. In the foreground, on top of Pilot Butte, is the road that circles around the butte to the top. Old maps show the river spelled with a capital C, originally two words, Des Chutes (in French, *the falls*). Photograph by William L. Van Allen; courtesy of his grandson William Thompson

X

1970-1983

These were the Nixon years. Elected in 1968 and taking office in January 1969, he had seen the final preparations for the first moon landing and talked with the first men on the moon, astronauts Neil A. Armstrong and Edwin E. Aldrin, Jr. Again, Pine Mountain observers watched Apollo 11 go out of sight, and NASA waited for their report. President Nixon's visit to China, China's acceptance in the United Nations, and the end of American participation in the war in Vietnam were overshadowed by Watergate. There was no loud shouting when the "boys" came home as there was after the armistice of the first World War. There was just patient waiting until these boys, grown into bitter men, were ready to talk.

Many of these veterans went back to school, taking high school equivalency tests before enrolling in Bend's Central Oregon Community College under the G.I. Bill. Brooks-Scanlon sold to the smaller Diamond Lumber Company that hired fewer men. Traffic was rushing through town on Highway 97, East Third Street, with drivers stopping only to eat at the many fast-food restaurants, shop in the new shopping centers, or sleep overnight in the motels with familiar names.

But Bend was being discovered again by Olympic hopefuls who found Mount Bachelor snow drier and longer-lasting than any other skiing area in the country, at affordable prices. Half a million skiers staying at Bend's motels and lodges in 1981 were a big boost to Bend's economy.

Senior citizens from other states are also finding Bend a pleasant place to retire. Three senior centers offer friendship, cards, dancing, crafts, and meals where they pay what they can afford. They also offer planned tours to other parts of the state and nearby attractions for anyone who doesn't prefer to spend his time fishing in the nearby Deschutes or playing golf at the Bend Golf Club.

And for the young people, there are jobs in nonpolluting industries or a chance to start a new industry using wood products.

Anyone who thinks East Third Street is all of Bend should follow the river at the Y when coming into town from the north, or return to the lights on Franklin if they have gone all the way through town. For there, after going under the railroad tracks, is the real Bend, the part that older settlers love and new settlers discover. There are Wall and Bond streets, Greenwood, Oregon, and Minnesota. Not an "Old Town" like many towns that have been passed by, but a busy, up-to-date shopping area where clerks are ready to wait on a customer or give a smiling invitation to look around. Here are restaurants where one feels like a guest that can tarry over a meal. Here on Wall Street is the city hall, the library, and the museum. A block off Wall Street is Drake Park, with benches, tables, and geese that come out to meet you. This is Bend in the heart of Bend country in central Oregon.

The Deschutes County Pioneer Association's first museum was purchased on May 1, 1971. It soon outgrew this small building on Greenwood, just off Bond Street, and members started looking around for larger quarters. Built in 1916, this building has housed many different occupants. It is believed that it was first a garage. Courtesy of William Van Allen collection

Hooter, who likes people and refuses to leave or hunt for himself when set free, enjoys many outings when Sunriver's resident naturalist/ecologist is invited by a Bend organization to talk about owls. He listens attentively and hoots appropriately, looking wise, knowing he is the main attraction. He is an interesting guest at many local organizational meetings. Courtesy of Sunriver Properties, Inc.

Each of Dorothy Vandevert's forty dolls is dressed in the material and style of dresses worn by wives and hostesses of each president on inauguration day. Even the faces and hair coloring of the dolls have been carefully selected to match, as closely as possible, the facial expressions, hair coloring, and style of the women they represent. She has also dressed over 150 dolls to be distributed in Christmas boxes. Courtesy of Dorothy Vandevert collection; photograph by Dave Swan, the *Bend Bulletin*

Romaine Village a mobile home park recreation hall, south of Bend, caters to the interests of its mobile home residents. Courtesy of Romaine Village

When Hattie Mayne retired from managing her nursing home, she went fishing. Courtesy of Violet Mayne Franks collection

Phil Brogan was the man behind the NBC national weather report from Bend for as long as BBC has been reporting the weather. His first job at the *Bend Bulletin* in 1923 was to check the weather from on top of the *Bend Bulletin* building, the job of every new man on the staff since 1903 when the *Bend Bulletin* first set up a press in the old log cabin. Time told Phil it was silly to climb that ladder, so the weather box was moved to his backyard.

Phil retired from the *Bulletin* after four decades of working, first as a reporter and then as an editor. He continued to write. His *East of the Cascades*, published in 1964, is an authorative reference about central Oregon's geology, paleontology, astronomy, and archeology.

When Phil and his wife Charlotte Harris Brogan moved to Denver to be near other members of the family, someone else had to take over the weatherman's job. Courtesy of *Bend Bulletin*, March 27, 1978

After many moves in rented quarters, Deschutes County finally built this beautiful, modern building in 1941. It dominates the low knoll north of Greenwood, on Bond Street. When this building was outgrown, an annex back of the courthouse replaced the old Central School and grounds.

While the author was attending Central School in the 1920s, she kept her horse in a small barn on or near the spot where the courthouse now stands. At noon, she watered her horse in the Deschutes below the Pilot Butte Inn. Courtesy of Kenneth Underhill

Beginning September 13th,
The Sunday Bulletin
A better way to enjoy your Sunday
THE BULLETIN

At last, after over three-quarters of a century, the *Bend Bulletin* announced that they would be putting out a Sunday paper instead of a Saturday paper. The daily paper came many years after the paper had been published only weekly, "A tri-weekly," many old-timers quipped. Courtesy of the *Bend Bulletin*, September 13, 1981

This gallery of discarded stuffed toys lined up to watch workers at Knotts' sanitary landfill outside Bend have been rescued by county employees to add a bit of humor to their work. The animals also amuse startled garbage haulers who see them for the first time. Courtesy of Virginia Colver Elliott; photograph from *Billings Gazette* in Montana

This is modern Greenwood in 1982, looking east from Wall Street to Bond Street. Greenwood ends at Wall Street where the Pilot Butte Inn forced a jog to the right, in the photograph, where Newport begins to cross the river. The Trailways bus station and restaurant buildings forced a move to the right in Greenwood. Eddie's (Williamson) Sales and Service Station cuts the corner on Greenwood and Wall Street, taking up half of both streets to the next corners. That isn't snow in the picture, it is Central Oregon sunshine.

When Eddie Williamson's parents decided to leave Bend in 1916, fifteen-year-old Eddie had a job at the Bend Garage for twenty-one dollars a week and elected to stay behind. From the author's collection

This is Eddy Williamson's corner that now runs all the way to Bond Street. Wall Street runs from left to right with a jog where Greenwood meets Newport at the lower left. Courtesy of Eddy Williamson

Eddie Williamson, a poor boy who came to Eugene from the Burns country in 1916, found a job in Walter Comb's garage for a few dollars a week. He decided to stay when his parents moved on. Here in the photo he is trying to persuade his friends Maurice Shelton, vice president of the First National Bank, (left) and Arthur Hill, tax accountant, (right), that it took all his money to buy in the Pilot Butte Inn at auction. Mrs. Hill taught school in Bend for thirty years before retiring. Courtesy of the Eddie Williamson collection

The Pilot Butte Inn was expensive to keep up. It began to run down, so it was put up for auction and sold. There was talk of it being used as a hotel or rooming house for senior citizens. Built in 1917, it wasn't old enough to be called a heritage building, but because of its fame, it was so designated. That didn't save it. It was sold again, and suddenly this bulldozer moved in and started to tear it down. Courtesy of Clyde McKay collection

This aerial view of Bend, taken in 1938, focuses along Greenwood to the bend in the river. The two big mills are out of sight toward the upper left. The footbridge is across the river from Drake Park. Newport Bridge is out of the picture toward the extreme right beyond the Pilot Butte Inn. From the author's collection

This aerial view is the center of Bend in 1972. Courtesy of Rose Hunnell collection

The curious llama is from the llama ranch at Sister, twenty-one miles from Bend. Courtesy of Cora Sather collection

This 1982 photograph of the Dr. Dean Masterson residence on Powers Road shows one of many successfully solar heated houses in the Bend country with its many sunshiny days. Even with snow on the ground it stays cozy warm with snow disappearing off the glass roof quickly. Courtesy of Mrs. Dean Masterson

This is the queen's table at the 1976 summer picnic in Pioneer Park. Seated at the table, from left to right, are: Nora Russell McMean, the 1970 queen; the author (1975), and Queen Violet Mayne Franks (1976). Next to the queen, going around the table is Ruth Almira Churche (Collver) Barnes (1974), Dorothy Brasel Vandevert (1972), and Agnes Grubb (1971). The selection of a new queen is kept a secret until the January meeting and party at the Pine Forest Grange hall. A pioneer queen has been selected every year since 1948. No queen was selected the first two years after the Deschutes Pioneer Association was organized. Courtesy of Judge Robert Foley

This is a list of the Deschutes Pioneers' past queens and presidents, from 1947 to 1980. Courtesy of the *Deschutes Pioneers' Gazette*

Deschutes Pioneers Past Queens and Presidents

	Queens	Presidents
1947 & 1948		Carl Johnson
1949	Mary Todd Bennett	E. A. Smith
1950	Pearl Vanderpool Becker	Edna Brinson
1951	Myrtle Sheperd Thompson	LeRoy Fox
1952	Anna Thompson	Claude Vandevert
1953	Addie Triplett	William J. Burton
1954	Luella Griffin	R. D. Ketchum
1955	Flossie Smith	Chester Springer
1956	Mary Kelley	Craig Coyner
1957	Elizabeth Bogue	Lowell Jensen
1958	Florence Spencer	Dean Hollinshead
1959	Mary Hoover	Robert Keyes
1960	Katie Ruble	Claude Kelley
1961	Belle Read	Claude Kelley
1962	Isa Corum Freeman	Steve Steidl
1963	Rose Gibson	D. Ray Miller
1964	Florence Stout	Antone Fossen
1965	Viola Logan	Cecil Moore
1966	Carrie Stevens	Ole Grubb
1967	Georgia Thom	C. L. Allen
1968	Minnie Helfrich	Reub Long
1969	Gracie Evans Grimes	Clarence Boyd
1970	Nora Russell McMeen	George Hostetler
1971	Agnes Grubb	Stanley Scott
1972	Dorothy Vandevert	Carol Boyd
1973	Eva Slack	Michael Mahoney
1974	Ruth Barnes	Mel Munkers
1975	Elsie Horn Williams	Mel Munkers
1976	Violet Mayne Franks	Rodney Rosebrook
1977	Martha Conklin	Ben Graffenberger
1978	Martha Long	Priday Holmes
1979	Elnora Dodson	Sam Johnson
1980	Sophia Becker Gibson	Alfred H. Triplett

In 1983 the Inn of Seventh Mountain is a popular resort of Olympic contestants since good skiing snow lasts long into the season after many other resorts are without skiing facilities. Summer vacationers find swimming, horseback riding, tennis, and a nice convention center here at reasonable costs, only seven miles southwest of Bend on a well paved road.

The seventh mountain is Bachelor Butte, over 9,000 feet high, and the seventh snowcapped peak in the Cascades south from Oregon's northern border.

The couple on the balcony are Jan and Kirk Sandburg. Kirk is the recreation director at Seventh Mountain Inn. Courtesy of the Seventh Mountain Inn

The Oregon High Desert Museum is a dream come true for Don Kerr, who thought, as a little child growing up in Portland, that it would be nice to have a little place for animals to come to, rather than to be caged, even though there was an attempt to duplicate their natural environment.

Coming to Central Oregon to get away from their jobs at the Washington Park Zoo, in Portland, Kerr and Bob Dahul, who were working on a master plan for the Portland Zoo, agreed that here was a place for their one-of-a-kind facility. Bend folks liked the idea, too, and money began coming in. One hundred dollars looked big in 1977, until larger contributions showed up, demanding matching money for land and a learning center, over a million dollars, before the grand opening, Sunday, May 30, 1982.

This is just the beginning. There are plans for an otter pond, a badger habitat, and porcupines. Birds and animals not usually found in this dry land have discovered the running stream and pool surrounded by native shrubs. Volunteer guides will explain native American craft, the trees and shrubs. Night animals might not be seen by the visitor, but a smoothed-off ground around the stream and path will show the prints of their feet when they come for water.

The museum is open every day except Thanksgiving, Christmas, and New Year's Day, from 9:00 a.m. to 5:00 p.m. It is a must stop among the several other points of interest just out of Bend.

Volunteer Jeff Cooney, with owl on hand, gives a public presentation of birds of prey, to an interested group. Courtesy of the Oregon Historical Desert Museum

Volunteers demonstrate pioneer skills in weaving. From left to right are Lena Myers, Ginger Shive, and Kathleen Couper. Courtesy of the Oregon High Desert Museum

The man is third generation pioneer Phil Chase of Tumalo. His audience includes (seated) Larry and Peter Chitwood, Tracyee Bowerman and Lisa Chitwood. Standing are Karen Chitwood and Jayson Bowerman. Courtesy of the Oregon High Desert Museum

Volunteer Bill McDonald introduces Governor Vic Atiyeh to a procupine on his visit to the Oregon High Desert Museum. Courtesy of the Oregon High Desert Museum

bibliography

A bibliography should give the sources of material used in a book so a reader can check the source for accuracy or to explore further into the subject. Several of the magazines from which I obtained quotes or pictures are out of print. Because of their age, they are now in the public domain.

These are:

Brooks-Scanlon's *Pine Echoes*

Motor Coach Age—given to author by Trailways

The Big Haul—U. S. Forest Service

The Oregon Builders, loaned by Dick Asseln, of Van Metre Construction Company.

The *Bulletin*, recently the *Bend Bulletin*, and the *Pioneers' Gazette* lay no claim to the pictures in their papers since they are now in the public domain. New pictures taken by their staff were freely offered to be used in this book.

Joyce Tifft Gribskov also loaned me prints used in her book *Pioneer Spirits of Bend*, and others were gathered from mutual friends.

about the author

Although Elsie Horn Williams has lived in Eugene, Oregon for over half a century, she still calls Bend her home town. Arriving in Bend in 1910, two years before the train, she went to Bend grade and high schools. She was married in Bend and had a daughter, their only child, before moving to the Willamette Valley.

She was a grandmother when she started college as a freshman, and graduated from the University of Oregon with a B.S. in sociology. "Not because I planned on getting a job as a social worker," she says, "except as a volunteer. No one will dare call me a 'sob sister' when I go to bat for some child or a group of children in need or in trouble." She has served on all levels from local to national in the American Legion's Children and Youth Programs, as a volunteer.

Majoring in sociology, she was able to delve in many subjects to broaden her education as a free-lance writer. She has sold poems, mostly humorous, to magazines and radio, and written short stories and articles. After appearing in a children's magazine, one of her children's stories has been reprinted in an Allen and Bacon Fifth Reader.

She says she is resisting writing articles as she wants to write something of more lasting value. She has traveled extensively in all fifty states and in Canada, researching for the nonfiction historical book she has been working on and hopes to have finished within the year.

"We, who have lived through most of this century, have a duty to preserve those years in books that tell it like it was instead of titillating fiction. We know the pictorial history of the Oregon country does that," she says.

index